THE WARS BETWEEN
ENGLAND AND AMERICA

THE
WARS BETWEEN
ENGLAND AND
AMERICA

BY

T. C. SMITH

PROFESSOR OF AMERICAN HISTORY IN WILLIAMS
COLLEGE, WILLIAMSTOWN MASS., U.S.A.

With an Introduction by
ELLIS A. JOHNSON
State University of New York

KENNIKAT PRESS/Port Washington, N.Y.

First printed 1914/15.

THE WARS BETWEEN ENGLAND AND AMERICA

First published 1914
Reissued 1969 by Kennikat Press

Library of Congress Catalog Card No: 68-26260
SBN 8046-0430-4
Manufactured in the United States of America

INTRODUCTION TO THE 1968 REISSUE

Those of us who view 1815 as a key year in American history certainly do not base our conclusion on anything transpiring therein; it stems, rather, from careful consideration of a great deal of what happened before and not a little of what was to come in the century immediately following. Here is a deceptively diminutive volume guaranteed to make a major part of the pre-1815 picture poignantly apparent. The Preface and Bibliography speak for themselves; my Bibliographical Note simply suggests, after a reference to Parkman which seems as mandatory as Mahan in any such undertaking, a few valuable sources which appeared since Smith's admirable study was originally brought out. That this was just as the first world war of our century exploded in the face of an idea of inevitable progress seems as symbolic as the closing words of Canada's great statesman sound appropriate. A century of peace between peoples *is*, as Sir Wilfred Laurier pointed out, "a spectacle to astound the world by its novelty and grandeur." That it was not always thus between British, Canadian, and

INTRODUCTION TO THE 1968 REISSUE

American is the burden of these dozen chapters surveying the scene across three thousand miles times time with an ease of style and sense of artistic restraint indicating the author's mastery of the tangled web from which they were spun.

Ellis Allen Johnson

State University of New York
College at Cortland
January, 1968

SUPPLEMENTARY BIBLIOGRAPHICAL NOTE

The incomparable conclusion of F. PARKMAN, *Montcalm and Wolfe*, chapt. xxxii, vol. ii (1885) sets the stage in terms of the triple kinship of laws, language, and blood. The Canadien-Canadian panorama from 1760 to confederation is presented by J. M. S. CARELESS in pt. iii of the deservedly popular *Canada: A Story of Challenge* (1963). Attitudes and events on both sides of the water are given comparably careful consideration by J. C. MILLER in *Origins of the American Revolution* (1943); the most moving follow-up, *Revolution 1776*, was subsequently issued as *A Short History of the American Revolution* by J. H. PRESTON (1933). In *The Reluctant Rebels* (1950), L. MONTROSS tells beautifully the story of the Continental Congress from 1774 to 1789, while C. VAN DOREN vividly details the making and ratifying of the Constitution of the United States in *The Great Rehearsal* (1948).

An American mosaic from colonial beginnings through the fiasco of 1812 emerges from a careful cross-hatching of four basic works: T. A. BAILEY, *A Diplomatic History of the American People* (1955), chapts. i-xii; A. C. McLAUGHLIN, *A Constitutional History of the United States* (1935), chapts. i-xxvii; W. BINKLEY, *American Political Parties: Their Natural History* (1949), chapts. i-vi; and R. A. BILLINGTON, *Westward Expansion: A History of the American Frontier* (1963), chapts. i-xiii. A triad of topical interpretation from Paris to Ghent may be built on K. FEILING, *A History of England from the Coming of the English to 1938* (1948), bk. vi; LORD ELTON, *Imperial Commonwealth: The History of Britain Through Its Three Great Periods* (1946), bks. v-viii; and, this above all, SIR W. S. CHURCHILL, *A History of the English Speaking Peoples* (1957), bks. viii-ix, vol. iii.

E. A. J.

PREFACE

The purpose of this volume is to show how social, economic, and political causes led to a period of almost continuous antagonism between England and the American communities from 1763 to the ratification of the Treaty of Ghent in 1815, and how that antagonism was ended. The war of American Independence, 1775–1783, and the war of 1812–1815 give their names to the book, not because of their military or naval importance, but because they mark, in each case, the outcome of successive years of unavailing efforts on the part of each country to avoid bloodshed. With this aim in view, no more detailed study of the internal political history or institutions of either country can be included than is necessary to account for different political habits; nor can the events of diplomatic history be developed beyond what is called for to explain persistent lines of action or the conclusion of a significant treaty.

CONTENTS

CHAP.		PAGE
I	THE ELEMENTS OF ANTAGONISM, 1763	9
II	THE CONTEST OVER PARLIAMENTARY TAXATION, 1763–1773	28
III	THE DISRUPTION OF THE EMPIRE, 1773–1776	51
IV	THE CIVIL WAR IN THE EMPIRE, 1776–1778	75
V	FRENCH INTERVENTION AND BRITISH FAILURE, 1778–1781	96
VI	BRITISH PARTIES AND AMERICAN INDEPENDENCE, 1778–1783	114
VII	THE FORMATION OF THE UNITED STATES, 1781–1793	129
VIII	THE FIRST PERIOD OF COMMERCIAL ANTAGONISM, 1783–1795	149
IX	THE TRIUMPH OF DEMOCRACY IN THE UNITED STATES, 1795–1805	169
X	THE SECOND PERIOD OF COMMERCIAL ANTAGONISM, 1805–1812	189
XI	THE WAR FOR "SAILORS' RIGHTS" AND WESTWARD EXPANSION, 1812–1815	215
XII	END OF THE ANTAGONISM: A CENTURY OF PEACE	236
	BIBLIOGRAPHY	251
	INDEX	254

THE WARS
BETWEEN
ENGLAND AND AMERICA

CHAPTER I

THE ELEMENTS OF ANTAGONISM, 1763

In 1763, by the Peace of Paris, England won a position of unapproached supremacy in colonial possessions and in naval strength. The entire North American continent east of the Mississippi River was now under the British flag, and four West India sugar islands were added to those already in English hands. In India, the rivalry of the French was definitely crushed and the control of the revenues and fortunes of the native potentates was transferred to the East India Company. Guided by the genius of Pitt, British armies had beaten French in Germany and America, and British fleets had conquered French and Spanish with complete ease. The power of the Empire seemed beyond challenge. Yet within this Empire itself there lay already the seeds of a discord which was soon to develop into an irrepressible contest, leading to civil war; then, for a generation, to drive the separated parts into renewed antagonism, and finally to cause a second war. Between the North American colonies and the mother country there existed such moral, political, and economic divergence that nothing but prudent and patient statesmanship on both sides of the Atlantic could prevent disaster.

The fundamental source of antagonism lay in the fact that the thirteen colonies had developed a wholly different social and political life from that of the mother country. Originally, the prevailing ideas and habits of the colonists and of the Englishmen who remained at home had been substantially the same. In England, as in America, the gentry and middle classes played a leading part during the years from 1600 to 1660. But by 1763 England, under the Hanoverian kings, had become a state where all political and social power had been gathered into the hands of a landed aristocracy which dominated the government, the Church, and the professions. In parliament, the House of Commons—once the body which reflected the conscious strength of the gentry and citizens,—had now fallen under the control of the peers, owing to the decayed condition of scores of ancient parliamentary boroughs. Nearly one-third of the seats were actually or substantially owned by noblemen, and of the remainder a majority were venal, the close corporations of Mayor and Aldermen selling freely their right to return two members at each parliamentary election. In addition, the influence and prestige of the great landowners were so powerful that even in the counties, and in those boroughs where the number of electors was considerable, none but members of the ruling class sought election. So far as the members of the middle class were concerned—the merchants, master weavers, iron producers, and craftsmen,—they were strong in wealth and their wishes counted heavily with the aristocracy in all legislation of a financial or commercial nature; but of actual part in the government they had none. As for the lower classes,—the labourers, tenant farmers, and shopkeepers,—they were able as a rule to influence government only by rioting and uproar. Without the ballot, they had no other way.

Owing to the personal weakness of successive monarchs since the death of William III, there had grown up the cabinet system of government which, in 1763, meant the reduction of the King to the position of an honorary figurehead and the actual control of officers, perquisites, patronage, and preferment, as well as the direction of public policy, by the leaders of parliamentary groups. The King was obliged to select his ministers from among the members of noble families in the Lords or Commons, who agreed among themselves after elaborate bargains and negotiations upon the formation of cabinets and the distribution of honours. In this way sundry great Whig family "connections," as they were called, had come to monopolize political power, excluding Tories, or adherents of the Stuarts, and treating government as solely a matter of aristocratic concern. Into this limited circle, a poor man could rise only by making himself useful through his talents or his eloquence to one of the ruling cliques, and the goal of his career was naturally a peerage.

The weakness of this system of government by family connection lay in its thorough dependence upon customs of patronage and perquisite. The public offices were heavily burdened with lucrative sinecures, which were used in the factional contests to buy support in Parliament, as were also peerages, contracts, and money bribes. When George III ascended the throne, in 1760, he found the most powerful Minister in the Cabinet to be the Duke of Newcastle, whose sole qualification, apart from his birth, was his pre-eminent ability to handle patronage and purchase votes. That such a system did not ruin England was due to the tenacity and personal courage of this aristocracy and to its use of parliamentary methods, whereby the orderly conduct of legislation and taxation and the habit of public attack and defence of government measures furnished political training for the whole ruling class. Further, the absence of any sharp caste lines made it possible for them to turn, in times of crisis, to such strong-fibred and masterful commoners as Walpole and Pitt, each of whom, in his way, saved the country from the incompetent hands of titled ministries.

This system, moreover, rested in 1763 on the aquiescence of practically all Englishmen. It was accepted by middle and lower classes alike as normal and admirable; and only a small body of radicals felt called upon to criticize the exclusion of the mass of taxpayers from a share in the government. Pitt, in Parliament, was ready to proclaim a national will as something distinct from the voice of the borough-owners, but he had few followers. Only in London and a few counties did sundry advocates of parliamentary reform strive in the years after 1763 to emphasize these views by organizing the freemen to petition and to "instruct" their representatives in the Commons. Such desires evoked nothing but contempt and antipathy in the great majority of Englishmen. Especially when they became audible in the mouths of rioters did they appear revolutionary and

14   THE WARS BETWEEN

obnoxious to the lovers of peace, good order, and the undisturbed collection of rents and taxes. Nothing but a genuine social revolution could bring such ideas to victory and that, in 1763, lay very far in the future. For the time conservatism reigned supreme.

In the thirteen colonies, on the other hand, the communities of middle-class Englishmen who emigrated in the seventeenth century had developed nothing resembling a real aristocracy. Social distinctions, modelled on those of the old country, remained between the men of large wealth—such as the great landed proprietors in New York and the planters in the South, or the successful merchants in New England and the Middle colonies—and the small farmers, shopkeepers, and fishermen, who formed the bulk of the population; while all of these joined in regarding the outlying frontiersmen as elements of society deserving of small consideration. Men of property, education, and " position " exercised a distinct leadership in public and private life. Yet all this remained purely social; in law no such thing as an aristocracy could be found, and in government the colonies had grown to be very nearly republican. Here lay the fundamental distinction between the England and the America of 1763. In America, a title or peerage conferred no political rights whatever; these were founded in every case on law, on a royal charter or a royal commission which established a frame of government, and were based on moderate property qualifications which admitted a majority of adult males to the suffrage and to office.

In every colony the government consisted of a governor, a council, and an assembly representing the freemen. This body, by charter, or royal instructions, had the full right to impose taxes and vote laws; and, although its acts were liable to veto by the governor, or by the Crown through the Privy Council, it possessed the actual control of political power. This it derived immediately from its constituents and not from any patrons, lords, or close corporations. Representation and the popular will were, in fact, indissolubly united.

The governor in two colonies, Connecticut and Rhode Island, was chosen by the freemen. Elsewhere, he was appointed by an outside authority: in Pennsylvania, Delaware, and Maryland by the hereditary proprietor to whom the charter had been granted, in all other colonies by the Crown. The councillors, who commonly exercised judicial functions in addition to their duties as the governor's advisers and as the upper house of the legislature, were appointed in all colonies except the three in New England;

and they were chosen in all cases from among the socially prominent colonists. The judges, also, were appointed by the governor; and they, with governor and council, were supposed to represent the home government in the colonies.

But in reality there was no effective imperial control. The Crown, it is true, appeared to have large powers. It granted charters, established provinces by commissions, exercised the right to annul laws and hear appeals from colonial decisions, exacted reports from governors, sent instructions, and made appointments and removals at will. But nearly all the colonial officials, except the few customs officers, were paid out of colonial appropriations, and this one fact sufficed to deprive them of any independent position. In nearly every colony, the assembly, in the course of two-thirds of a century of incessant petty conflict, of incessant wrangling and bargaining, of incessant encroachments on the nominal legal powers of the governor, had made itself master of the administration. The colonists resisted all attempts to direct their military or civil policy, laid only such taxes as they chose, raised only such troops as they saw fit, passed only such laws as seemed to them desirable, and tied the governor's hands by every sort of device. They usurped the appointment of the colonial treasurer, they appointed committees to oversee the expenditure of sums voted, they systematically withheld a salary from the governor, in order to render him dependent upon annual " presents," liable to diminution or termination in case he did not satisfy the assembly's wishes. The history of the years from 1689 to 1763 is a chronicle of continual defeat for governors who were obliged to see one power after another wrenched away from them. Under the circumstances, the political life of the thirteen colonies was practically republican in character, and was as marked for its absence of administrative machinery as the home government was for its aristocracy and centralization.

Another feature of colonial life tended to accentuate this difference. Although religion had ceased to be a political question, and the English Church was no longer regarded, save in New England, as dangerous to liberty, the fact that the great majority of the colonists were dissenters—Congregational, Presbyterian, or Reformed, with a considerable scattering of Baptists and other sects—had an effect on the attitude of the people toward England. In the home country, the controlling social classes accepted the established church as part of the constitution; but in the colonies it had small strength, and even where it was by law established it remained little more than an official body, the "Governor's church." This tended to widen the gap between the political views of the individualistic dissenting and Puritan sects in the colonies and the people at home.

The American of 1763 was thus a different kind of man from the Englishman. As a result of the divergent development on the two sides of the Atlantic from a common ancestry, their political habits had become mutually incomprehensible. To the Englishman, the rule of the nobility was normal—the ideal political system. He was content, if a commoner, with the place assigned to him. To the colonist, on the other hand, government in which the majority of adult male inhabitants possessed the chief power was the only valid form,—all others were vicious. Patriotism meant two contradictory things. The Englishman's patriotism was sturdy but unenthusiastic, and showed itself almost as much in a contempt for foreigners as in complacency over English institutions. The colonist, on the contrary, had a double allegiance: one conventional and traditional, to the British crown; the other a new, intensely local and narrow attachment to his province. England was still the "old home," looked to as the source of political authority, of manners and literature. It was for many of the residents their recent abode and, for all except a few of Dutch, German, or French extraction, their ancestral country. But already this "loyalty" on the part of the colonists was dwindling into something more sentimental than real. The genuine local patriotism of the colonists was shown by their persistent struggle against the representatives of English authority in the governors' chairs. There had developed in America a new sort of man, an "American," who wished to be as independent of government as possible, and who, while professing and no doubt feeling a general loyalty to England, was in fact a patriot of his own colony.

The colonists entered very slightly into the thoughts of the English noblemen and gentry. They were regarded in a highly practical way, without a trace of any sentiment, as members of the middle and lower classes, not without a large criminal admixture, who had been helped and allowed to build up some unruly and not very admirable communities. Nor did the English middle classes look upon the colonists with much interest, or regard them as, on the whole, their equals. The prevailing colonial political habits, as seen from England, suggested only unwarrantable wrangling indicative of political incompetence and a spirit of disobedience. Loyalty, to an Englishman, meant submission to the law. To men trained in such different schools, words did not mean the same thing. The time had come when the two peoples were scarcely able to understand each other.

A second cause for antagonism, scarcely less fundamental and destined to cause equal irritation, is to be found in the conflict between the economic life of the American communities and the beliefs of the mother country concerning commercial and naval policy. Great Britain, in 1763, was predominantly a trading country. Its ships carried goods for all the nations of Europe and brought imports to England from all lands. Although the manufacturers were not yet in possession of the new inventions which were to revolutionize the industries of the world, they were active and prosperous in their domestic production of hardware and textiles, and they furnished cargoes for the shipowners to transport to all quarters. To these two great interests of the middle classes, banking and finance were largely subsidiary. Agriculture, the mainstay of the nobility and gentry, continued to hold first place in the interests of the governing classes, but the importance of all sources of wealth was fully recognized.

In the colonies, on the contrary, manufacture scarcely existed beyond the domestic production of articles for local use; and the inhabitants relied on importations for nearly all finished commodities and for all luxuries. Their products were chiefly things which Great Britain could not itself raise, such as sugar in the West Indies; tobacco from the islands and the southern mainland colonies; indigo and rice from Carolina; furs, skins, masts, pine products; and, from New England, above all, fish. The natural market for these articles was in England or in other colonies; and in return British manufactures found their natural market in the new communities. When the Economic Revolution transformed industry, and factories, driven by steam, made England the workshop of the world, the existing tendency for her to supply America with manufactured products was intensified regardless of the political separation of the two countries. Not until later economic changes supervened was this normal relationship altered.

The traditional British policy in 1763 was that of the so-called Mercantile System, which involved a thoroughgoing application of the principle of protection to the British shipowner, manufacturer, and corn-grower against any competition. An elaborate tariff, with a system of prohibitions and bounties, attempted to prevent the landowner from being undersold by foreign corn, and the manufacturer from meeting competition from foreign producers. Navigation Acts shut out foreign-built, -owned, or -manned ships from the carrying trade between any region but their home country and England, reserving all other commerce for British vessels. Into this last restriction there entered another purely political consideration, namely, the perpetuation of a supply of mariners for the British navy, whose importance was fully recognized. So far as the colonies were concerned, they were brought within the scope of mercantilist ideas by being considered as sources of supply for England in products not possible to raise at home, as markets which must be reserved for British manufacturers and traders, and as places which must not be allowed to develop any rivalry to British producers. Furthermore, they were so situated that by proper regulations they might serve to encourage British shipping even if this involved an economic loss.

The Navigation Acts accordingly, from 1660 to 1763, were designed to put this theory into operation, and excluded all foreign vessels from trading with the colonies, prohibited any trade to the colonies except from British ports and enumerated certain commodities—sugar, cotton, dye woods, indigo, rice, furs—which could be sent only to England. To ensure the carrying out of these laws, an elaborate system of bonds and local duties was devised, and customs officers were appointed, resident in the colonies, while governors were obliged to take oath to enforce the Acts. As time revealed defects or unnecessary stringencies, the restrictions were frequently modified. The Carolinas, for instance, were allowed to ship rice not only to England, but to any place in Europe south of Cape Finisterre. Bounties were established to aid the production of tar and turpentine; but special Acts prohibited the export of hats from the colonies, or the manufacture of rolled iron, in order to check a possible source of competition to British producers. In short, the Board of Trade, the administrative body charged with the oversight of the plantations, devoted its energies to suggesting devices which should aid the colonists, benefit the British consumer and producer, and increase " navigation."

It does not appear that the Acts of Trade were, in general, a source of loss to the colonies. Their vessels shared in the privileges reserved for British-built ships. The compulsory sending of the enumerated commodities to England may have damaged the tobacco-growers; but in other respects it did little harm. The articles would have gone to England in any case. The restriction of importation to goods from England was no great grievance, since British products would, in any case, have supplied the American market. Even the effort, by an Act of 1672, to check intercolonial trade in enumerated commodities was not oppressive, for, with one exception noted below, there was no great development of such a trade. By 1763, according to the best evidence, the thirteen colonies seem to have adjusted their habits to the Navigation Acts, and to have been carrying on their flourishing commerce within these restrictions.

To this general condition, however, there were some slight exceptions, and one serious one. The colonists undoubtedly resented the necessity of purchasing European products from English middlemen, and were especially desirous of importing Spanish and Portuguese wines and French brandies directly. Smuggling in these articles seems to have been steadily carried on. Much more important—and to the American ship-owners the kernel of the whole matter—was the problem of the West India trade. It was proved, as the eighteenth century progressed, that the North American colonies could balance their heavy indebtedness to the mother country for excess of imports over exports only by selling to the French, as well as the British West Indies, barrel staves, clapboards, fish and food products. In return, they took sugar and molasses, developing in New England a flourishing rum manufacture, which in turn was used in the African slave trade. By these means the people of the New England and Middle colonies built up an active commerce, using their profits to balance their indebtedness to England. This " triangular trade " disturbed the British West India planters, who, being largely non-residents and very influential in London, induced Parliament, in 1733, to pass an Act imposing prohibitory duties on all sugar and molasses of foreign growth. This law, if enforced, would have struck a damaging blow at the prosperity of the Northern colonies, merely to benefit the West India sugar-growers by giving them a monopoly; but the evidence goes to show that it was systematically evaded and that French sugar, together with French and Portuguese wines, was still habitually smuggled into the colonies. Thus the Navigation Acts, in the only points where they would have been actually oppressive, were not enforced. The colonial governors saw the serious consequences and shrank from arousing discontent. It is significant that the same colonists who contended with the royal governors did not hesitate to violate a parliamentary law when it ran counter to their interests.

The only reason why the radical difference

between the colonies and the home government did not cause open conflict long before 1763 is to be found in the absorption of the English ministries in parliamentary manœuvring at home, diplomacy, and European wars. The weakness of the imperial control was recognized and frequently complained of by governors, Boards of Trade, and other officials; but so long as the colonies continued to supply the sugar, furs, lumber and masts called for by the Acts, bought largely from English shippers and manufacturers, and stimulated the growth of British shipping, the Whig and Tory noblemen were content. The rapidly growing republicanism of the provincial and proprietary governments was ignored and allowed to develop unchecked. A half-century of complaints from thwarted governors, teeming with suggestions that England ought to take the government of the colonies into its own hands, produced no results beyond creating in official circles an opinion unfavourable to the colonists.

In the years of the French war, 1754–1760, the utter incompatibility between imperial theories on the one hand and colonial political habits on the other, could no longer be disregarded. In the midst of the struggle, the legislatures continued to wrangle with governors over points of privilege; they were slow to vote supplies; they were dilatory in raising troops; they hung back from a jealous fear that their neighbour colonies might fail to do their share; they were ready to let British soldiers do all the hard fighting. Worse still, the colonial shipowners persisted in their trade with the French and Spanish West Indies, furnishing their enemies with supplies, and buying their sugar and molasses as usual. When, in Boston, writs of assistance were employed by the customs officials, in order that by a general power of search they might discover such smuggled property, the merchants protested in the courts, and James Otis, a fiery young lawyer, boldly declared the writs an infringement of the rights of the colonists, unconstitutional, and beyond the power of Parliament to authorize. To Ministers engaged in a tremendous war for the overthrow of France, the behaviour of the colonies revealed a spirit scarcely short of disloyalty, and a weakness of government no longer to be tolerated. The Secretaries, the Board of Trade, the customs officials, army officers, naval commanders, colonial governors, and judges all agreed that the time had come for a thorough and drastic reform. They approached the task purely and simply as members of the English governing classes, ignorant of the colonists' political ideas and totally indifferent to their views; and their measures were framed in the spirit of unquestioning acceptance of the principles of the Acts of Trade as a fundamental national policy.

CHAPTER II

THE CONTEST OVER PARLIAMENTARY TAXATION, 1763–1773

THE Prime Minister responsible for the new colonial policy was George Grenville, who assumed his position in May, 1763, shortly after the final treaty of Paris. Every other member of his Cabinet was a nobleman, Grenville himself was brother of an earl, and most of them had had places in preceding Ministries. It was a typical administration of the period, completely aristocratic in membership and spirit, quite indifferent to colonial views, and incapable of comprehending colonial ideals even if they had known them. To them the business in hand was a purely practical one; and with confident energy Grenville pushed through a series of measures, which had been carefully worked out, of course, by minor officials unknown to fame, during the preceding months,

ENGLAND AND AMERICA 29

but which were destined to produce results undreamed of by any one in England.

In the first place, there were a number of measures to strengthen and revivify the Acts of Trade. Colonists were given new privileges in the whale fishery, hides and skins were "enumerated," and steps were taken to secure a more rigorous execution of the Acts by the employment of naval vessels against smuggling. A new Sugar Act reduced the tariff on foreign sugar to such a point that it would be heavily protective without being prohibitive, and at the same time imposed special duties on Portuguese wines, while providing additional machinery for collecting customs. This was clearly aimed at the weak point in the existing navigation system; but it introduced a new feature, for the sugar duties, unlike previous ones, were intended to raise a revenue, and this, it was provided in the Act, should be used to pay for the defence of America.

A second new policy was inaugurated in a proclamation of October, 1763, which made Florida and Canada despotically governed provinces, and set off all the land west of the head-waters of the rivers running into the Atlantic as an Indian reservation. No further land grants were to be made in that region, nor was any trade to be permitted with the Indians save by royal licence. The

Imperial government thus assumed control of Indian policy, and endeavoured to check any further growth of the existing communities to the West. Such a scheme necessitated the creation of a royal standing army in America on a larger scale than the previous garrisons; and this plan led to the third branch of the new policy, which contemplated the positive interposition of Parliament to remedy the shortcomings of colonial assemblies. An Act of 1764 prohibited the future issue of any paper money by any colony, thus terminating one of the chief grievances of British governors and merchants. But still more striking was an Act of 1765, which provided with great elaboration for the collection of a stamp tax in the colonies upon all legal documents, newspapers, and pamphlets. The proceeds were to be used to pay about one-third of the cost of the new standing army, which was to consist of ten thousand men. Taken in connection with the announced intention of using the revenue from the Sugar Act for the same purpose, it is obvious that Grenville's measures were meant to relieve the Imperial government from the necessity of depending in future upon the erratic and unmanageable colonial legislatures. They were parts of a general political and financial programme. There is not the slightest evidence that Grenville or his associates dreamed

ENGLAND AND AMERICA

that they were in any way affecting the colonists' rights or restricting their liberties. Grenville did consult the colonial agents—individuals authorized to represent the colonial assemblies in England—but simply with a view to meeting practical objections. The various proclamations or orders were issued without opposition, and the bills passed Parliament almost unnoticed. The British governing class was but slightly concerned with colonial reform: the Board of Trade, the colonial officials, and the responsible Ministers were the only people interested.

To the astonishment of the Cabinet and of the English public, the new measures, especially the Sugar Act and the Stamp Act, raised a storm of opposition in the colonies unlike anything in their history. The reasons are obvious. If the new Sugar Act was to be enforced, it meant the end of the flourishing French West India intercourse and the death of the " triangular " trade. Every distiller, shipowner, and exporter of fish, timber, or grain, felt himself threatened with ruin. If the Stamp Act were enforced, it meant the collection of a tax from communities already in debt from the French wars, which were in future to be denied the facile escape from heavy taxes hitherto afforded by bills of credit. But the economic burdens threatened were almost lost sight of in the political dangers. If England meant to impose taxes by parliamentary vote for military purposes, instead of calling upon the colonists to furnish money and men, it meant a deadly blow to the importance of the assemblies. They could no longer exercise complete control over their property and their finances. They would sink to the status of mere municipal bodies. So far as the Americans of 1765 were concerned, the feeling was universal that such a change was intolerable, that if they ceased to have the full power to give or withhold taxes at their discretion they were practically slaves.

In every colony there sprang to the front leaders who voiced these sentiments in impassioned speeches and pamphlets; for the most part young men, many of them lawyers accustomed to look for popular approval in resisting royal governors. Such men as James Otis and Samuel Adams in Massachusetts, William Livingston in New York, Patrick Henry in Virginia, Christopher Gadsden in South Carolina denounced the Stamp Act as tyrannous, unconstitutional, and an infringement of the liberties of the colonists. Popular anger rose steadily until, in the autumn, when the stamps arrived, the people of the thirteen colonies had nerved themselves to the pitch of refusing to obey the Act. Under pressure from crowds of angry men,

ENGLAND AND AMERICA 33

every distributor was compelled to resign, the stamps were in some cases destroyed, and in Boston the houses of unpopular officials were mobbed and sacked. Before the excitement, the governors stood utterly helpless. They could do nothing to carry out the Act.

In October, delegates representing nearly all the colonies met at New York, and drafted resolutions expressing their firm belief that no tax could legally be levied upon them but by their own consent, given through their legislatures. It was the right of Englishmen not to be taxed without their consent. Petitions in respectful but determined language were sent to the King and to Parliament, praying for the repeal of the Stamp Act and the Sugar Act. For the first time in their history, the colonies stood together in full harmony to denounce and reject an Act passed by Parliament. As a social and political fact, this unanimous demonstration of colonial feeling was of profound significance. The ease and ability with which the lawyers, planters, farmers, or merchants directed the popular excitement into effective channels showed the widespread political education of the Americans. A not dissimilar excitement in London in the same years found no other means of expressing itself than bloody rioting. It was American republicanism showing its strongest aspect in political resistance.

The issue thus presented to the British government was one demanding the most careful consideration and far-seeing wisdom in its treatment. Grenville's measures, however admirable and reasonable in themselves, had stirred the bitter opposition of all the colonists, and the enforcement or modification of them called for steadiness and courage. Were the English governing noblemen of the day ready to persist in the new policy? If so, it meant violent controversy and possibly colonial insurrection; but the exertion of British authority, if coupled with strong naval pressure, ought to prevail. Angry as the colonists were, their language indicates that revolution was not in their thoughts; and, if there was one quality beyond all others in which the British aristocracy excelled, it was an inflexible tenacity when once a policy was definitely embraced. Unfortunately for both sides, the clear-cut issue thus raised was obscured and distorted by the presence on the throne of an ambitious young prince with a policy which threw British domestic affairs into unexampled confusion.

George III, obstinate, narrow-minded, and determined to make his own will felt in the choice of Ministers and the direction of affairs, had succeeded his grandfather in 1760. Too astute to violate the fast-bound tradition of the British constitution that he must govern only through Ministers, he saw that to have his own way he must secure political servants who, while acting as Cabinet Ministers, should take their orders from him. He also saw that to destroy the hold of the Whig family cliques he must enter politics himself and buy, intimidate, and cajole in order to win a following for his Ministers in parliament. With this ideal in view, he subordinated all other considerations to the single one of getting subservient Ministers, and fought or intrigued against any Cabinet which did not accept his direction, until, in 1770, he finally triumphed. In the meantime he had kept England under a fluctuating succession of Ministries which forbade the maintenance of any coherent or authoritative colonial policy such as alone could have prevented disaster.

In 1761 George III tried to induce Parliament to accept the leadership of the Earl of Bute, his former tutor, who had never held public office; but his rapid rise to the Premiership aroused such jealousy among the nobility and such unpopularity among the people that the unfortunate Scot quailed before the storm of ridicule and abuse. He resigned in 1763, and was succeeded by Grenville, who instantly showed George III that he would take no dictation. On the contrary, he drove the King to the point of fury by his masterfulness. In desperation, George then turned to the Marquis of Rockingham who, if equally determined to decline royal dictation, was personally less offensive to him; and there came in a Ministry of the usual type, all noblemen but two minor members, and all belonging to " connections " different from those of the Grenville Ministry. Thus it was that, when the unanimous defiance of the Americans reached England, the Ministers responsible for the colonial reforms were out of office, and the Rockingham Whigs had assumed control, feeling no obligation to continue anything begun by their predecessors. George III's interposition was responsible for this situation.

When Parliament met in January, 1766, the colonists received powerful allies, first in the British merchants, who petitioned against the Act as causing the practical stoppage of American purchases, and second in William Pitt, who, in a burning speech, embraced in full the colonists' position, and declared that a parliamentary tax upon the plantations was absolutely contrary to the rights of Englishmen. He " rejoiced that America has resisted." This radical position found few followers; but the Whig Ministry, after some hesitation, decided to grant the colonial demands while insisting on the imperial rights of Parliament. This characteristically English action was highly distasteful to the majority in the House of Lords, who voted to execute the law, and to George III, who disliked to yield to mutinous subjects; but they were forced to give way. The Stamp Act was repealed, and the sugar duties were reduced to a low figure. At the same time a Declaratory Act was passed, asserting that Parliament had full power to bind the colonies "in all cases whatsoever." Thus the Americans had their way in part, while submitting to seeing their arguments rejected.

The consequences of this unfortunate affair were to bring into sharp contrast the British and the American views of the status of the colonies. The former considered them as parts of the realm, subject like any other part to the legislative authority of King, Lords, and Commons. The contention of the colonists, arising naturally from the true situation in each colonial government, that the rights of Englishmen guaranteed their freedom from taxation without representation, was answered by the perfectly sound legal assertion that the colonists, like all the people of England, were "virtually" represented in the House of Commons. The words, in short, meant one thing in England, another thing in America. English speakers and writers pointed to the scores of statutes affecting the colonies, calling attention especially to the export duties of the Navigation Act of 1672, and the import duties of the Act of 1733, not to mention its revision of 1764. Further, Parliament had regulated provincial coinage and money, had set up a postal service, and established rates. Although Parliament had not imposed any such tax as the Stamp Act, it had, so far as precedent showed, exercised financial powers on many occasions.

To meet the British appeal to history, the colonists developed the theory that commercial regulation, including the imposition of customs duties, was "external" and hence lay naturally within the scope of imperial legislation, but that "internal" taxation was necessarily in the hands of the colonial assemblies. There was sufficient plausibility in this claim to commend it to Pitt, who adopted it in his speeches, and to Benjamin Franklin, the agent for Pennsylvania, already well known as a "philosopher," who expounded it confidently when he was examined as an expert on American affairs at the bar of the Commons. It was, however, without any clear legal justification, and, as English speakers kept pointing out, it was wholly incompatible with the existence of a genuine imperial government. That it was a perfectly practical distinction, in keeping with English customs, was also true; but that was not to be realized until three-quarters of a century later.

With the repeal of the objectionable law the uproar in America ceased, and, amid profuse expressions of gratitude to Pitt, the Ministry, and the King, the colonists returned to their normal activities. The other parts of the Grenville programme were not altered, and it was now possible for English Ministers, by a wise and steady policy, to improve the weak spots in the colonial system without giving undue offence to a population whose sensitiveness and obstinate devotion to entire self-government had been so powerfully shown. Unfortunately, the King again interposed his influence in such wise as to prevent any rational colonial policy. In the summer of 1766, tiring of the Rockingham Ministry, he managed to bring together an odd coalition of political groups under the nominal headship of the Duke of Grafton. Pitt, who disliked the family cliques, accepted office and the title of Earl of Chatham, hoping to lead a national Ministry. The other elements were in part Whig, and in part representatives of the so-called " King's Friends "—a growing body of more or less venal politicians who clung to George's support for the sake of the patronage to be gained — and several genuine Tories who looked to a revived royal power to end the Whig monopoly. From such a Cabinet no consistent policy was to be expected, save under leadership of a man like Pitt. Unfortunately the latter was immediately taken with an illness which kept him out of public life for two years; and Grafton, the nominal Prime Minister, was utterly unable to hold his own against the influence and intrigues of the King. From the start, accordingly, the Ministry proved weak and unstable, and it allowed a new set of colonial quarrels to develop.

Charles Townshend, Chancellor of the Exchequer, one of the originators of the new colonial policy under the Bute Ministry, was so ill-advised as to renew the attempt to raise a colonial revenue by parliamentary taxation. His manner of proposing the measure gave the impression that it was a piece of sheer bravado on his part, intended to regain the prestige which he had lost by failing to carry all of his first budget; but the nature of the scheme indicates its close connection with the Grenville ideals. Avoiding the appearance of a direct internal tax, he caused the imposition of duties on glass, painters' colours, paper, and tea, without any pretence of regulating commerce, but for the announced purpose of defraying the expenses of governors and judges in the colonies. Another measure established an American Board of Commissioners for customs. Still another punished the province of New York for failing to comply with an Act of 1765 authorizing quartering of troops in the colonies. The assembly was forbidden to pass any law until it should make provision for the soldiers in question. Ex-governor Pownall of Massachusetts, now in Parliament, did not fail to warn the House of the danger into which it was running; but his words were unheeded, and the Bills passed promptly.

The result of these measures was inevitable. Every political leader in the colonies —nay, every voter—saw that the Townshend duties, while in form "external," were pure revenue measures, unconnected with the Acts of Trade, and intended to strike at colonial independence in a vital point. If Great Britain undertook henceforward to pay the salaries of royal officials, one of the principal sources of power would be taken away from the assemblies. Instantly the distinction of "external" and "internal" taxation was abandoned; and from end to end of the Atlantic seaboard a cry went up that the duties were an insidious attack on the liberties of the Americans, an outrageous taking of their property without their consent, and a wanton interference with their governments. Not merely agitators such as the shrewd Samuel Adams and the eloquent Patrick Henry uttered these views, but men of far more considerable property and station— such as John Jay and New York landowners and importers, John Dickinson and the Philadelphia merchants, George Washington and the Virginia planters. While no general Congress was summoned, the legislatures of the colonies adopted elaborate resolutions, pamphleteers issued a stream of denunciations, and, most important of all, a concerted effort was made to break down the Acts by abstaining from any importations, not only of the taxed commodities, but, so far as possible, of any British products. Commercial boycott, it was hoped, would have the same effect as at the time of the Stamp Act.

By this time the colonial argument had come to assume a much broader character, for, in order to deny the validity of the New York Assembly Act and the Townshend duties, it became necessary to assert that Parliament, according to "natural rights," had no legislative authority over the internal affairs of a colony. This was vested, by the constitution of each province or chartered colony, in the Crown and the colonial legislature. Such a theory reduced the imperial tie to little more than a personal union through the monarch, coupled with the admitted power of Parliament to regulate commerce and navigation. Evidently, as in all such cases, the theory was framed to justify a particular desire, namely, to keep things where they had been prior to 1763. The sole question at issue was, in reality, one of power, not of abstract or legal right.

Once more it was clear to men of penetrating vision that the American colonies needed extremely careful handling. Whether their arguments were sound or fallacious, loyal or seditious, it was significant that the whole continent spoke with one voice and felt but one desire—to be allowed to exercise complete financial discretion and to retain full control over governors and judges. Unfortunately the condition of things in England was such that a cool or steady treatment of the question was becoming impossible. In the first place, the Grafton Ministry was reconstituted in 1768, the "Pittite" elements withdrawing, and being replaced by more King's Friends and Tories, while George III's influence grew predominant. Townshend died in September, 1767, but his place was taken by Lord North, a Tory and especially subservient to the King. A new secretaryship for the colonies was given to Lord Hillsborough, who had been in the Board of Trade in the Grenville Ministry, and represented his views. Neither of these men was inclined to consider colonial clamour in any other light than as unpardonable impudence and sedition. In the second place, the old Whig family groups were fast assuming an attitude of bitter opposition to the new Tories, and by 1768 were prepared to use the American question as a convenient weapon to discredit the Ministry. They were quite as aristocratic in temper as the ministerial party, but advocated forbearance, conciliation, and calmness in dealing with the Americans, in speeches as remarkable for their political good sense as for their ferocity toward North, Hillsborough, and the rest. While the Ministry drew its views of the American situation from royal governors and officials, the Whigs habitually consulted with Franklin and the other colonial agents, who occupied a quasi-diplomatic position. Thus the American question became a partisan battleground. The Tories, attacked by the Whigs, developed a stubborn obstinacy in holding to a " firm " colonial policy, and exhibited a steady contempt and anger toward their American adversaries which was in no small degree due to the English party antagonism.

Still further to confuse the situation, there occurred at this time the contest of John Wilkes, backed by the London mob, against the Grafton Ministry. This demagogue, able

ENGLAND AND AMERICA 45

and profligate, had already come into conflict with the Grenville Ministry in 1765, and had been driven into exile. Now, in 1768, he returned and was repeatedly elected to the Commons, and as often unseated by the vindictive ministerial majority. Riots and bloodshed accompanied the agitation; and Wilkes and his supporters, backed by the parliamentary Whigs, habitually proclaimed the same doctrines of natural rights which were universally asserted in America. To the King and his Cabinet, Wilkes and the American leaders appeared indistinguishable. They were all brawling, disorderly, and dangerous demagogues, deserving of no consideration.

Under these circumstances, the complaints of the colonists, although supported by the Whigs and by Chatham, received scant courtesy in England. The Grafton Ministry showed nothing but an irritated intention to maintain imperial supremacy by insisting on the taxes and demanding submissiveness on the part of the assemblies. A series of " firm " instructions was sent out by Hillsborough, typical of which was an order that the Massachusetts legislature must rescind its circular letter of protest under threat of dissolution, and that the other assemblies must repudiate the letter under a similar menace. The sole result was a series of embittered wrangles, dissolutions, protests, and quarrels which left the colonists still more inflamed. Then, at the suggestion of the Commissioners of Customs, two regiments of troops were sent to Boston to overawe that particularly defiant colony. There being no legislature in session, the Massachusetts towns sent delegates to a voluntary convention which drafted a protest. Immediately, this action was denounced by Hillsborough as seditious and was censured by Parliament; while the Duke of Bedford moved that an old statute of Henry VIII, by which offenders outside the realm could be brought to England for trial, should be put into operation against the colonial agitators. When the Virginia legislature protested against this step, it was dissolved. Hillsborough and North acted as though they believed that a policy of scolding and nagging, if made sufficiently disagreeable, would bring the colonists to their senses. That the Whigs did not cease to pour contempt and ridicule on the folly of such behaviour was probably one reason why the government persisted in its course. The American question was coming to be beyond the reach of reason.

Yet in 1769 the Ministry could not avoid recognizing that as financial measures the Townshend duties were a hopeless failure, since their net proceeds were less than £300 and the increased military expenses were declared by Pownall to be over £170,000. On May 1, 1769, the Cabinet voted to repeal the taxes on glass, colours, and paper, but by a majority of one determined to keep the tea duty. This decision was due to the complaisance of Lord North, who saw the unwisdom of the step, but yielded to the King's wish to retain one tax in order to assert the principle of parliamentary supremacy. A year later, the Grafton Ministry finally broke up; and Lord North assumed control, with a Cabinet composed wholly of Tories and supported by George III to the full extent of his power, through patronage, bribes, social pressure, and political proscription. North himself was inclined to moderation in colonial matters. He carried the promised repeal of all the duties but the tea tax, and in 1772 replaced the arrogant and quarrelsome Hillsborough with the more amiable Lord Dartmouth. It looked for a while as though the political skies might clear, for the American merchants, tired of their self-imposed hardships, began to weaken in opposition. In 1769 the New York assembly voted to accept the parliamentary terms; and in 1770 the merchants of that colony voted to abandon general non-importation, keeping only the boycott on tea. This led to the general collapse of the non-importation agreements; but the colonial temper continued to be defiant and suspicious, and wrangling with governors was incessant.

Occasional cases of violence confirmed the English Tories in their low view of the Americans. In March, 1770, a riot in Boston between town rowdies and the soldiers brought on a shooting affray in which five citizens were killed. This created intense indignation throughout the colonies, regardless of the provocation received by the soldiers, and led to an annual commemoration of the "Boston Massacre," marked by inflammatory speeches. The soldiers, however, when tried for murder in the local courts, were defended by prominent counsel, notably John Adams, and were acquitted. Two years later, on June 9, 1772, the *Gaspee*, a naval schooner, which had been very active in chasing smugglers in Rhode Island waters, was burned by a mob, and its captain taken prisoner. The utmost efforts of the home government failed to secure the detection or punishment of any one of the perpetrators.

Finally, in December, 1773, a still more serious explosion occurred. The North Ministry, desirous of assisting the East India Company, which was burdened with debt, removed practically all restrictions on the exportation of tea to America in hopes of increasing the sale by reducing the price. To the colonial leaders, now in a state of chronic irritation, this measure seemed an insulting and insidious attempt to induce the Americans to forget their principles and buy the tea because it was cheap. It was denounced from end to end of the country in burning rhetoric; and when the cargoes of tea arrived their sale was completely prevented by the overwhelming pressure of public opinion. Consignees, waited on by great crowds, hastened to resign; and the tea was either seized for nonpayment of duties and allowed to spoil, or was sent back. In Boston, however, the Governor, Hutchinson, stiffly refused to let the tea ships depart without landing the tea, whereat the exasperated citizens watched an organized mob of disguised men board the ships and throw the tea into the harbour. Once more the unanimous voice of the colonies defied a parliamentary Act.

Such was the situation in 1773. Thirteen groups of British colonists, obstinately local in their interests, narrowly insistent on self-government, habituated to an antagonistic attitude toward royal governors, but, after all has been said, unquestionably loyal to the Crown and the home country, had been transformed into communities on the verge of permanent insubordination. Incapable of changing all their political habits, they could see in the British policy only a purpose to deprive them of that self-government which was inseparable from liberty. The Crown Ministers, on the other hand, unable to discover anything illegal, oppressive, or unreasonable in any of their measures, found no explanation of the extravagant denunciations of the colonial radicals other than a determination to foment every possible difficulty with a view to throwing off all obedience. While Adams, Dickinson, Henry, Gadsden and the rest demanded their "rights," and protested against "incroachments" on their liberties, Bedford, Hillsborough, North, and Dartmouth insisted on the "indecency," "insolence," and "disloyalty" shown by the Americans. The colonial republicans and the British noblemen were unable to speak the same language. Yet the time had come to face the situation, and it was the duty of the Ministers to assume the task with something more serious than reproofs and legal formulæ. The contest for power now begun must lead, unless terminated, straight to a disruption of the Empire.

CHAPTER III

THE DISRUPTION OF THE EMPIRE, 1773–1776

WHEN the news reached England that the people of the town of Boston had thrown the tea of the East India Company into the harbour, the patience of the North ministry, already severely strained, reached an end. Its members felt—and most of the English people felt with them—that to submit to such an act of violence was impossible. Every consideration of national dignity demanded that Boston and its rioters should be punished, and that the outrage done to the East India Company should receive atonement. Hitherto, they said, the contumacious colonists had been dealt with chiefly by arguments, reproofs, and, as it seemed to most Englishmen, with concessions and kindnesses which had won only insult and violence.

It was resolved to make an example of the delinquent community; and the first step was to humiliate its representative, Benjamin Franklin. Ever since 1765 he had been residing in England, respected as a philosopher and admired as a wit, bearing a sort of diplomatic character through his position as agent for the assemblies of Massachusetts, Pennsylvania, and Georgia. In close association with the Whig opposition, he was undoubtedly the best-known American, and among the most influential. Now, in 1774, having to present a petition from Massachusetts to the Privy Council for the removal of Lieutenant-Governor Hutchinson, Franklin found it an awkward feature of the case that the colony's charges were based on private letters which he himself had in some way acquired and sent to Boston. The Court party determined to crush him, and at the hearing put forward Wedderburn, the Solicitor-General—a typical King's Friend—who passed over the subject of the petition to brand Franklin in virulent invective as a thief and scoundrel. Amidst general applause, the petition was rejected as false and scandalous, and Franklin was dismissed from his position of colonial Postmaster-General.

When Parliament met, it was instantly made clear that the sole idea controlling King, Cabinet, and the majority of Members was to bring the Massachusetts colonists to their senses by severe punitive legislation. The Whig opposition did not attempt to defend the destruction of the tea; but it spared no effort to make the Ministers see the folly of striking at effects and ignoring causes. In a masterly speech of April 19, 1774, Burke showed that the insistence on submission regardless of the grievances and of the nature

ENGLAND AND AMERICA 53

of the colonists was a dangerous and absurd policy, and Pownall and Chatham repeated his arguments, but without avail. The Ministerial party saw no danger, and felt nothing but the contempt of an irritated aristocracy. The original ideals of a general colonial reform were now lost sight of; the men responsible for them had all passed off the stage; Grenville, Townshend, and Halifax were dead, and North, careless and subservient to George III, Hillsborough, Suffolk, Sandwich, and Rochford—all noblemen, and in many cases inefficient—did not see beyond the problem of coercing noisy and troublesome rioters, indistinguishable from the followers of Wilkes. Over and over again they reiterated that the colonists' resentment was not to be feared, that they would submit to genuine firmness, that they were all cowardly and dared not resist a few regular troops. Lord George Germaine earned the thanks of Lord North by declaring that the colonists were only " a tumultuous and noisy rabble," men who ought to be " following their mercantile employment and not attempting to govern." Not a gleam of any other statesmanship appears in any of the Ministerial speeches than that displayed in the determination to exact complete submission.

There were passed, accordingly, by the full Ministerial majority, five measures known as the Coercive Acts, or, in America, as the Five Intolerable Acts. The first one punished Boston by closing the port to all trade until the offending town should recompense the East India Company for the tea destroyed. The next altered the government of Massachusetts Bay by making the councillors appointive instead of elective, by placing the appointment and removal of all judicial officers entirely in the hands of the governor, by placing the selection of jurors in the hands of the sheriffs and prohibiting town-meetings —apart from the annual one to elect officers— without the governor's permission. A third Act authorized the transfer to England for trial of British officers charged with murder committed while in discharge of their duties. A fourth Act re-established the system of quartering troops.

The fifth Act reorganized the province of Quebec, whose government, under the Proclamation of 1763, had proved defective in several respects. The legal institutions of the new colony were not well adapted to the mixed French and British inhabitants, and the religious situation needed definition. The Quebec Act altered the government of the province by the creation of an appointive council, authorized the Catholic Church to collect tithes, and allow the French to substitute an oath of allegiance for the oath of supremacy. Moreover, French civil law was permitted to exist. At the same time the boundaries of the province were extended into the region west of the mountains so as to include the lands north of the Ohio River.

With the passage of these Acts, the original causes for antagonism were superseded. The commissioners of customs might have enforced the Navigation Acts indefinitely; the objectionable Tea Act might have stood permanently on the statute-book; but, without a more tangible grievance, it is not easy to conceive of the colonists actually beginning a revolution. The time had now come when a more serious issue was raised than the right of Parliament to collect a revenue by a tariff in the colonies. If Parliament was to be allowed to crush the prosperity of a colonial seaport, to centralize a hitherto democratic government created by a royal charter, and to remove royal officers from the scope of colonial juries, it was clear that the end of all the powers and privileges wrung from royal or proprietary governors by generations of struggle was at hand. Yet the striking feature in this punitive legislation was that the North Ministry expected it to meet no resistance, although its execution, so far as the government of Massachusetts was concerned, rested on the consent of the colonists. There was, under the British system, no administrative body capable of carrying out these laws, no military force except the few regiments in Boston, and no naval force beyond a few frigates and cruisers. The mere passage of the laws, according to North and to Lord Mansfield, was sufficient to bring submission.

Nothing more clearly shows the profound ignorance of the Tory Ministry than this expectation, for it was instantly disappointed. At the news of the Acts, the response from America was unanimous. Already the colonial Whigs were well organized in committees of correspondence, and now they acted not merely in Massachusetts but in every colony. The town of Boston refused to vote compensation, and was immediately closed under the terms of the Port Act. Expressions of sympathy and gifts of provisions came pouring into the doomed community; while public meetings, legislatures, political leaders and clergymen, in chorus denounced the Acts as unconstitutional, cruel, and tyrannous. The Quebec Act, extending the Catholic religion and French law into the interior valley under despotic government, was regarded as scarcely less sinister than the Regulating Act itself.

Under the efficient organization of the leaders a Continental Congress met in Philadelphia in October, 1774, to make united

ENGLAND AND AMERICA 57

protest. This body, comprising without exception the most influential men in the colonies, presented a clear contrast to Parliament in that every man was the representative of a community of freemen, self-governing and equal before the law. The leaders did not regard themselves in any sense as revolutionaries. They were simply delegates from the separate colonies, met to confer on their common dangers. Their action consisted in the preparation of a petition to the King, addresses to the people of England, the people of Quebec, and the people of the colonies, but not to Parliament, since they denied its right to pass any such laws as those under complaint. The Congress further drew up a declaration of rights which stated sharply the colonial claims, namely, that Parliament had no right to legislate for the internal affairs of the separate colonies. It also adopted a plan for putting commercial pressure on England by forming an Association whose members pledged themselves to consume no English products, and organize committees in every colony to enforce this boycott. The leaders in the body were destined to long careers of public prominence—such men as George Washington, Lee, and Patrick Henry of Virginia, Rutledge of South Carolina, Dickinson of Pennsylvania, Jay of New York, Samuel and John Adams of Massachusetts. They differed considerably in their temper, the Massachusetts men being far more ready for drastic words and deeds than the others; but they held together admirably. If such protests as theirs could not win a hearing in England, it was hardly conceivable that any could.

Meanwhile the situation gave signs of being more explosive in reality than the respectful words of the Congress implied. In Massachusetts, the town of Boston showed no sign of submitting, and endured distress and actual starvation, although much cheered by gifts of food from all parts of the continent. The new government under the Regulating Act proved impossible to put into operation, for the popular detestation was visited in such insulting and menacing forms that the new councillors and judges dared not serve. More radical action followed. When Gage, having caused the election of a legislature, prorogued it before it had assembled, the members none the less gathered. Declaring that the Regulating Act was invalid, they elected a council, appointed a committee of safety, and named a receiver of taxes. On February 1, 1775, a second Provincial Congress was chosen by the towns, which had not even a nominal sanction by the governor. The colony was, in fact, in peaceful revolution, for Gage found himself unable to collect taxes or to make his authority respected as governor beyond the range of his bayonets. Equally significant was it that in several other colonies, where the governors failed to call the legislatures, provincial congresses or conventions were spontaneously elected to supervise the situation and choose delegates to the Continental Congress.

So deep was the popular anger in Massachusetts Bay that the collection of arms and powder and the organization of militia were rapidly begun. Clearly, the Massachusetts leaders were preparing to persist to the verge of civil war. But by this time there began to be felt in the colonies a countercurrent of protest. As the situation grew darker, and men talked openly of possible separation unless the intolerable wrongs were redressed, all those whose interests or whose loyalty revolted at the idea of civil war became alarmed at the danger. Soon men of such minds began to print pamphlets, according to the fashion of the time, and to attempt to prevent the radicals from pushing the colonies into seditious courses. But the position of these conservatives was exceedingly difficult, for they were obliged to apologize for the home country at a time when every act on the part of that country indicated a complete indifference to colonial prejudices. Their arguments against revolution or independence left, after all, no alternative except submission. Denounced as Tories by the hotter radicals, they found themselves at once more and more alarmed by the daring actions of the Whigs, and more detested by the excited people of their communities.

The action of the British government after these events showed no comprehension of the critical situation into which they were rushing. George III and North secured in the election of 1774 a triumphant majority of the Commons, and felt themselves beyond reach of danger at home. The arguments of the colonists, the protests of the Continental Congress, fell upon indifferent ears. Although Burke and Chatham exerted themselves with astonishing eloquence in the session of Parliament which began in November 1774, the Whig motions for conciliation were voted down by the full Ministerial majority. Petitions from merchants, who felt the pressure of the Non-importation Association, were shelved. So far as the policy of the Ministry may be described, it consisted of legislation to increase the punishment of Massachusetts Bay and extend it to other colonies, and to offer a conditional exemption from Parliamentary taxation. Both houses of Parliament declared Massachusetts Bay to be in rebellion, and voted to

ENGLAND AND AMERICA

crush all resistance. An Act was passed on March 30, to restrain the trade of New England, shutting off all colonial vessels from the fisheries, and forbidding them to trade with any country but England or Ireland. By a second Act, in April, this restriction was extended to all the colonies except New York and Georgia. The only purpose of this Act was punitive. Every step was fought by the Whig opposition, now thoroughly committed to the cause of the colonists, but their arguments had the inherent weakness of offering only a surrender to the colonists' position which the parliamentary majority was in no mood to consider. In fact it was only with great difficulty and after a stormy scene that North induced his party to vote a so-called conciliatory proposition offering to abstain from taxing any colony which should make such a fixed provision for civil and judicial officers as would satisfy Parliament.

It was only a few days after the passage of the restraining Acts by Parliament that the long-threatened civil war actually broke out in Massachusetts. General Gage, aware of the steady gathering of powder and war material by the revolutionary committee of safety, finally came to the conclusion that his position required him to break up these threatening bases of supplies. On April 19, 1775, he sent out a force of 800 men to

Lexington and Concord—towns a few miles from Boston—with orders to seize or destroy provisions and arms. They accomplished their purpose, after dispersing with musketry a squad of farmers at Lexington, but were hunted back to Boston by many times their number of excited "minute men," who from behind fences and at every crossroad harassed their retreat. A reinforcement of 1500 men enabled the raiding party to escape, but they lost over 300 men, and inflicted a total loss of only 90 in their flight.

Thus began the American Revolution, for the news of this day of bloody skirmishing, as it spread, started into flame the excitement of the colonial Whigs. From the other New England colonies men sprang to arms, and companies marched to Boston, where they remained in rude blockade outside the town, unprovided with artillery or military organization, but unwilling to return to their homes. From the hill-towns, a band of men surprised Fort Ticonderoga on Lake Champlain, taking the cannon for use around Boston. In every other colony militia were organized, officers chosen and arms collected, and almost everywhere, except in Quaker Pennsylvania and in proprietary Maryland, the governors and royal officials fled to the seacoast to take refuge in royal ships of war, or resigned their positions at the command

ENGLAND AND AMERICA

of crowds of armed "minute men." Conventions and congresses, summoned by committees of safety, were elected by the Whigs and assumed control of the colonies, following the example of Massachusetts. The British colonial government, in short, crumbled to nothing in the spring of 1775. Only Gage's force of a few regiments, shut up in Boston, and a few naval vessels, represented the authority of England in America.

Again there met a Continental Congress at Philadelphia, whose duty it was to unify colonial action and to give the colonial answer to the late parliamentary acts. Once more the ablest men of the colonies were present, now gravely perturbed over the situation, and divided into two camps. On the one hand, most of the New Englanders, led by Samuel Adams and John Adams, his cousin, felt that the time for parley was at an end, that nothing was to be hoped for from the North Ministry, and that the only reasonable step was to declare independence. Others still hoped that George III would realize the extent of the crisis and be moved to concessions, while yet others, who hoped little, thought that one more effort should be made to avoid revolution. But none dreamed of surrender. Of the growing number of Americans who recoiled in horror from the possibility of independence, and were beginning to show their dread in every way, not one was in this body. It represented only the radicals in the several colonies.

The Congress has been charged with inconsistency, for some of its measures were impelled by the most radical members, others by the conservatives. On the one hand, it declined to adopt a form of federation suggested by Franklin, and authorized Dickinson to draw up a final, respectful, almost obsequious petition to the King to avoid war—a document called the "Olive Branch"; but, on the other hand, it appointed Washington to command the troops near Boston as a Continental commander, adopted a report censuring the conciliatory proposition in bold language, and issued an address justifying with extravagant rhetoric the taking up of arms. Still more daring, it went so far as to arrange to pay the so-called "Continental army" by means of bills of credit, redeemable by the united colonies. Later, in 1775, it appointed a secret committee to correspond with friends abroad, and undertook extensive measures for raising troops and accumulating military stores. To the revolted colonies, who found themselves with no legal authorities, it gave the advice to form such governments as would secure peace and good order during the continuance

ENGLAND AND AMERICA

of the existing dispute, a step which was promptly taken by several.

Fighting meanwhile went on. General Gage, on June 17, undertook to drive from Charlestown, across the harbour from Boston, a body of about 1,500 provincial troops who had intrenched themselves on Breed's Hill. In all, about 3,000 British were brought to the attack, while gunboats raked the peninsula between Charlestown and the mainland, hindering the arrival of reinforcements. With true British contempt for their adversaries, the lines of red-uniformed troops marched under the hot sun up the hill, to be met with a merciless fire at short range from the rifles, muskets, and fowling pieces of the defenders. Two frontal attacks were thus repelled with murderous slaughter; but a third attack, delivered over the same ground, was pushed home, and the defenders were driven from their redoubt. Never was a victory more handsomely won or more dearly bought. The assailants lost not less than 1,000 out of 3,000 engaged, including 92 officers. The Americans lost only 450, but that was almost as large a proportion. It was obvious to any intelligent officer that the Americans might have been cut off from behind and compelled to surrender without being attacked; but Gage and his subordinates were anxious to teach the rebels a lesson. The result of this action, known in history as "Bunker Hill," was to render him and nearly all the officers who served against Americans unwilling ever again to storm intrenchments. They discovered that, as Putnam, who commanded part of the forces, observed, the militia would fight well if their legs were covered. They were later to discover the converse, that with no protection militia were almost useless.

From this time the British force remained quietly in Boston, fed and supplied from England at immense cost, and making no effort to attack the miscellaneous levies which General Washington undertook to form into an army during the summer and autumn. Nothing but the inaction of the British made it possible for Washington's command to remain, for they lacked powder, bayonets, horses and, most serious of all, they lacked all military conceptions. The elementary idea of obedience was inconceivable to them. Washington's irritation over the perfectly unconcerned democracy of the New Englanders was extreme; but he showed a wonderful patience and tenacity, and by sheer persistence began to create something like a military organization. Yet, even after months of drill and work the army remained little more than an armed mob. At length, in March, 1776, Washington managed to place a force on Dorchester heights, which commanded the harbour from the south. At first Gage had some idea of attacking, but storms intervened; and finally, without another blow, he evacuated the city and sailed with all his force to Halifax. So ended a siege which ought never to have lasted a month had the British generals been seriously minded to break it up.

Other military events consisted of a few skirmishes in Virginia and North Carolina, where the governors managed to raise small forces of loyalists, who were thoroughly defeated by the Whig militia, and of a gallant but hopeless attempt by the rebels to capture Canada. After some futile efforts on the part of Congress to induce the French to revolt, two bodies of men, in the autumn of 1775, made their way across the border. One, entering Canada by way of Lake Champlain, occupied Montreal, and then advanced against Quebec, where it was joined by the other, which, with great hardships, had penetrated through the wilderness of northern Maine. The commanders, Richard Montgomery, Benedict Arnold, and Daniel Morgan of Virginia, were men of daring, but their force, numbering not more than 1,000, was inadequate; and, after the failure of an effort to carry the place by surprise on the night of December 31—in which Montgomery was killed and Morgan captured—they were unable to do more than maintain a blockade outside the fortress.

The action of the North Ministry during these months showed no deviation from its policy of enforcing submission. The Olive Branch petition was refused a reception, and a proclamation was issued declaring the colonies in rebellion and warning all subjects against traitorous correspondence. When Parliament met in November, 1775, the opposition, led as usual by Burke, made one more effort to avoid civil war; but the Ministerial party rejected all proposals for conciliation, and devoted itself to preparing to crush the rebellion. On December 22, an Act became law which, if enforced, would have been a sentence of death to all colonial economic life. It superseded the Boston Port Act and the restraining Acts, absolutely prohibited all commerce with the revolted colonies, and authorized the impressment into the navy of all seamen found on vessels captured under the Act.

Military and naval preparations were slow and costly. The Admiralty and War Office, unprepared for a general war, had insufficient troops and sailors, and had to collect or create supplies and equipment. The Earl of Sandwich showed activity but slight capacity as First Lord of the Admiralty. Viscount

Barrington had been Secretary at War under Pitt during the French war, but he lacked force and influence. Hence, although Parliament voted 50,000 troops, there was confusion and delay. To secure a prompt supply of men, the Ministry took the step of hiring German mercenaries from the lesser Rhine princes—Hesse, Waldeck, and others, —at a rate per head with a fixed sum for deaths. This practice was customary in wars when England was obliged to protect Hanover from the French; but to use the same method against their own kindred in America was looked upon with aversion by many English, and aroused ungovernable indignation in all Americans. It seemed to show a callousness toward all ties of blood and speech which rendered any hope of reconciliation futile. The war was not, in fact, popular in England. The task of conquering rebels was not relished by many, and officers and noblemen of Whig connections in some cases resigned their commissions rather than serve. The parliamentary opposition denounced the war with fiery zeal as an iniquity and a scandal. Nevertheless, the general opinion in England supported the Ministry in its determination to assert the national strength; for the colonial behaviour seemed to the average Englishman as nothing more or less than impudent sedition, to yield to which would be disgrace.

To the Americans, the British action in 1776 showed that the only alternatives were submission or fighting; and, if the latter must be chosen, then it was the feeling of a growing number that independence was the only outcome. There now went on a contest between conservatives, including on one side those who opposed all civil war, those who were willing to fight to defend rights but who were unwilling to abandon hopes of forcing England to surrender its claims, and those whose businesses and connections were closely interwoven with the mother country and all the radicals on the other. Unfortunately for the conservatives they had only fear, or sentiment, for arguments, since the North Ministry gave them nothing to urge upon doubtful men. Still more unfortunately, they were, as a rule, outside the revolutionary organizations of conventions and committees, and were themselves without means of co-operating.

In the excitement and tension of the time, the ruder and rougher classes tended to regard all reluctance to join in the revolution as equivalent to upholding the North policy, and to attack as Tories all who did not heartily support the revolutionary cause. Violence and intimidation rapidly made themselves felt. Loyalists were threatened, forced by mobs to sign the Association; their houses

ENGLAND AND AMERICA

were defiled, their movements watched. Then arms were taken from them, and if they showed anger or temper they were occasionally whipped or even tarred and feathered. In this way a determined minority backed by the poorer and rougher classes, overrode all opposition and swelled a rising cry for independence.

The Congress was slow, for it felt the need of unanimity; and such colonies as New York and Pennsylvania were controlled by moderates. But at length, in June, 1776, spurred on by the Virginia delegates and by the tireless urgings of the Massachusetts leaders, the body acted. Already some of the colonies had adopted constitutions whose language indicated their independence. Now the Continental Congress, after a final debate, adopted a Declaration of Independence, drafted by Jefferson of Virginia and supported by the eloquence of John Adams and the influence of Franklin. Basing their position on the doctrines of the natural right of men to exercise full self-government and to change their form of government when it became oppressive, the colonies, in this famous document, imitated the English Declaration of Rights of 1689 in drawing up a bill of indictment against George III's government. In this can be discovered every cause of resentment and every variety of complaint which the thirteen colonies were ready to put forward. Practically all were political. There were allusions in plenty to the wrangles between governors and assemblies, denunciations of the parliamentary taxes and the coercing Acts, but no reference to the Acts of Trade. To the end, the colonists, even in the act of declaring independence, found their grievances in the field of government and not in economic regulation. What they wanted was the unrestricted power to legislate for themselves and to tax or refrain from taxing themselves. When these powers were diminished, their whole political ideal was ruined, and they preferred independence to what they considered servitude. Such ideas were beyond the comprehension of most Englishmen, to whom the whole thing was plain disloyalty, however cloaked in specious words and glittering generalities.

It has been said that the rupture was due to a spirit of independence in America which, in spite of all disclaimers, was determined to be entirely free from the mother country. Such was the assertion of the Tories and officials of the time, and the same idea is not infrequently repeated at the present day. But the truth is that the colonists would have been contented to remain indefinitely in union with England, subjects of the British crown, sharers of the British commercial empire, provided they could have been sure of complete local self-government. The independence they demanded was far less than that now enjoyed by the great colonial unions of Canada, Australia, and South Africa. It may be assumed, of course, that unless Parliament exercised complete authority over internal as well as external matters—to employ the then customary distinction—there was no real imperial bond. Such was the position unanimously taken by the North Ministry and the Tories in 1776. But in view of the subsequent history of the English colonies it seems hardly deniable that some relationship similar to the existing colonial one might have been perpetuated had the Whig policy advocated by Burke been adopted, and the right of Parliament " to bind the colonies in all cases whatsoever " been allowed to drop, in practice. The obstinate localism of the colonies was such that not until a generation after the Revolution did a genuine American national sentiment appear. The colonies were driven to act together in 1774–1776, but not to fuse, by a danger not to national but to local independence. This fact indicates how sharply defined was the field which the Americans insisted on having free from parliamentary invasion. Had it been possible for England to recognize this fact, there would have been no revolution.

It is, of course, obvious that the traditional American view of the Revolution as caused by tyranny and oppression is symbolical, if not fictitious. The British government, in all its measures, from 1763 to 1774, was moderate, hesitating, and at worst irritating. Its action threatened to destroy the practical independence of the colonial assemblies; but the danger was political. Even the five " intolerable Acts " inflicted hardship on the town of Boston alone. It was not until the year 1775, when Parliament imposed severe commercial restrictions, that anything resembling actual oppression began; but by that time the colonies were in open revolt.

This fact only emphasizes, as Burke pointed out, the criminal folly of the North Ministry in allowing the situation to become dangerous. It was the misfortune of the British people in the eighteenth century that, in the critical years after 1767, George III and his Ministers were unable to conceive of any value in colonies which were not in the full sense dependencies, and were narrowly limited by the economic ideas of their time and the social conventions of their class. Since the colonies had developed, unchecked, their own political life under British government, it was not their duty humbly to surrender all that had come to be identical with liberty in their eyes. It was the duty of British statesmen to recognize the situation and deal with it. This they failed to do, and the result was revolution.

CHAPTER IV

THE CIVIL WAR IN THE EMPIRE, 1776–1778

In the war which now began, the military situation was such that neither side could look forward to an easy victory. Great Britain outweighed the colonies in population by three or four to one, and in every element of military strength to a much greater degree. There was a standing army, an ample sufficiency of professional officers, the most powerful navy in the world, the full machinery of financial administration, abundant credit, and wealthy manufacturing and agricultural classes which has already shown their power to carry the burdens of a world contest without flinching. With a powerful party Ministry endowed with full discretion in the ordering of military affairs, there was little danger of divided councils or of inability to secure responsible direction. North, Sandwich at the Admiralty, Barrington as Secretary at War, Germaine as Secretary for the Colonies, could command the active support of the King, the Parliament, and, it appeared, of the people.

On the other hand, it was necessary to carry on war at 3,000 miles distance from the base of supplies, and to feed and clothe the armies entirely from home. The cost was certain to be extremely heavy, and the practical difficulties of management arising from the distance were sure to be great, unless a competent commander were to be given complete authority in the colonies. Then, too, the problem was not one of conquering cities or single strategic points, or of defeating a rival state, but of so thoroughly beating down resistance as to lead the Americans to abandon their revolution and submit to the extinction of their new-formed confederation. Armies must operate inland from a seacoast where landing was easy in hundreds of places, but where almost every step took them into a rough country, ill-provided with roads and lacking in easily collected supplies. In spite of all advantages of military power, the problem before the British government was one calling for the highest forms of military capacity, and this, by an unexplained ill-fortune, was conspicu-

ENGLAND AND AMERICA 77

ously lacking. Not a British general who commanded in America failed to show fighting ability and tactical sense, but not one of them possessed the kind of genius which grasps the true military ends of any campaign and ignores minor points for the sake of winning decisive advantages. Perhaps it would be unjust to apply to the British forces in this war the designation won in 1774—"armies of lions led by asses"; but the analogy is at least suggested.

Still more serious was the fact that the North Ministry was chosen mainly on the basis of the willingness of its members to execute the King's orders and use their influence and parliamentary power and connections in his behalf. North himself, able as a parliamentarian, was irresolute in policy, ignorant of war, and careless in administration; Weymouth and Suffolk, the Secretaries, were of slight ability; Lord George Germaine, Secretary for the Colonies, was arrogant, careless, and lacking in military insight; Barrington, Secretary at War, possessed administrative ability, but was without personal weight in the cabinet; Sandwich at the Admiralty was grossly inefficient. There was not a single member of the Cabinet fitted to carry on war, or able to influence George III. For such a body of men to undertake to direct the operations in America at the distance of 3,000 miles was a worse blunder than it would have been to commit the conduct of the war to any one of the generals in the field, however commonplace his abilities.

On the side of the colonists, the problem of fighting the full power of England was apparently a desperate one. The militia, with superior numbers, had chased the British from Concord, and had made a stubborn defence at Bunker Hill; but the British were about to move with overwhelming strength. To raise, equip, clothe, and feed armies was the task of a strong administration, and there was nothing of the kind in America. The ex-colonists not only had never known efficient administration; they had fought against any and all administration for generations, and their leaders had won their fame as opponents of all executive power. To thunder against royal oppression won applause, but indicated no ability at raising money and organizing such things as commissariat, artillery, or a navy; and it may be said of such men as Samuel Adams, Robert Morris, Roger Sherman, John Rutledge, Patrick Henry, and Thomas Jefferson that their administrative training was as far below that of their enemies in the North Ministry as their political capacity was, in general, superior.

The Continental Congress, moreover, which assumed responsibility for the army, could only recommend measures to the States, and call upon them to furnish troops and money. In contrast to the States, which derived their powers unquestionably from the voters within their boundaries and could command their obedience, the Congress had no legal or constitutional basis, and was nothing more than the meeting place of delegates from voluntary allies. Such military authority as it exercised rested entirely upon the general agreement of the States. National government, in short, did not exist. Still more serious was the fact that there were very few trained officers in America. The American military leaders, such as Washington, Greene, Wayne, Sullivan, were distinctly inferior in soldiership to their antagonists, although Washington and Greene developed greater strategic ability after many blunders. It was only through sundry military adventurers, some English—such as Montgomery, Gates, Lee, Conway, — others European — such as De Kalb, Steuben, Pulaski—that something of the military art could be acquired.

Most serious of all, there were no troops in America who comprehended the nature of military discipline. The conception of obedience to orders, of military duty, of the absolute necessity of holding steady, was beyond the range of most Americans. They regarded war as something to be carried on in their own neighbourhoods, and resisted obstinately being drawn outside their own States. They refused to enlist for longer than a few months, since they felt it imperative to return to look after their farms. They had little regard for men from different districts, distrusted commanders from any State but their own, and had no loyalty of any description to the Continental Congress. They were, in short, still colonists, such as generations of training had made them; very angry with Great Britain, infuriated at Tories, and glad to be independent, but unable to realize the meaning of it all even under the terrible stress of war.

Under the circumstances, the task of the men to whose lot it fell to lead the American forces was such as to tax to the utmost not only their military skill, but their ability to control, inspire, and persuade the most refractory and unreliable of material. When to this were added the facts that the colonies were almost wholly lacking in manufactures except of the most rudimentary sort, that they had little capital except in the form of land, buildings, vessels, and crops, and that whatever revenue they had been in the habit of deriving from commerce was

ENGLAND AND AMERICA 81

liable to be destroyed by the British naval supremacy, it is easily seen that the disadvantages of the home country were actually counterbalanced by the still more crushing disadvantages of the revolting colonies.

In the summer of 1776, the British advanced from two quarters. In the north, as soon as navigation opened, men-of-war sailed up the St. Lawrence and brought reinforcements to Quebec. The relics of the American force, unable to maintain themselves in Canada, abandoned their conquests without a blow, and retreated into the Lake Champlain region, there intending to hold the forts at Crown Point and Ticonderoga. Col. Guy Carleton, the new commander, was soon able to move southward with overwhelming numbers; but, after reaching the northern end of Lake Champlain, he found that body of water commanded by a small squadron of gunboats under Benedict Arnold, and, deeming it impossible to advance, delayed all summer in order to construct a rival fleet. Meanwhile, all operations came to a standstill in that region. Eleven thousand men, chiefly regular troops, were thus kept inactive for months.

The principal British force gathered at Halifax, and sailed directly against New York. It was there joined by the remains of a naval expedition which had endeavoured in June,

1776, to capture Charleston, South Carolina, but had suffered severely in an attempt to bombard Fort Moultrie and been compelled to withdraw. This success, which raised the spirits of the rebels, was, however, the last they were to enjoy for many months. The main British expedition was expected to overpower all colonial resistance, for it comprised a fleet of men-of-war, and an army of no less than 31,000 men, including German mercenaries, fully equipped, drilled, and provisioned. The admiral in command, Lord Howe, a Whig, was authorized to issue pardons in return for submission, and evidently expected the mere presence of so powerful an armament to cause the collapse of all resistance. His brother, Sir William Howe, who commanded the army, was a good officer in actual fighting, but a man of little energy or activity, and unwilling, apparently, to cause the revolted colonies any more suffering than was necessary. He was, moreover, quite without military insight of the larger kind, failing to recognize the peculiar character of the war upon which he was entering and acting, when pushing on a campaign, precisely as though he were operating against a European army in west Germany.

In spite of all deficiencies, it seemed as though Howe could not fail to crush the undisciplined collection of 17,000 militia and minute men with which Washington endeavoured to meet him at New York. Controlling the harbour and the rivers with his fleet, he could move anywhere and direct superior numbers against any American position. The first blow, struck after futile efforts at negotiation, was aimed at an American force which held Brooklyn Heights on Long Island. About 20,000 British and Hessian troops were landed on August 22; and five days later they outflanked and crushed a body of Americans placed to obstruct their advance. There remained the American intrenchments, which were weak and ill-defended; but Howe refused to attack, probably with memories of Bunker Hill in his mind. Washington managed, owing to favourable rainy weather, to remove his beaten force by night on August 29, but only the inaction of Howe enabled them to escape capture.

There followed a delay of two weeks, during which Admiral Howe tried to secure an interview with American leaders, in hopes of inducing the rebels to submit; but, finding Franklin, Adams and Rutledge—commissioners named by Congress—immovably committed to independence, he was compelled to renew hostilities. There ensued a slow campaign in which General Howe easily forced Washington to evacuate New York, to retreat northward, and after various skirmishes to withdraw over the Hudson River into New Jersey. At no time did Washington risk a general engagement; at no time did he inflict any significant loss upon his antagonist or hinder his advance. The militia were, in fact, almost useless in the open field, and only dared linger before the oncoming redcoats when intrenched or when behind walls and fences. Many of them from New England grew discouraged and homesick, and left the moment their short enlistments expired; so that without any serious battles Washington's so-called army dwindled week by week. On November 16, a severe loss was incurred through the effort of General Greene to hold Fort Washington, which commanded the Hudson River from the heights at the northern end of Manhattan Island. This stronghold, besieged by Howe, made a fair defence, but was taken by storm, and the whole garrison captured. The American army then, in two detachments under Washington and Lee respectively, was obliged to retreat across New Jersey, followed by the British under Cornwallis, until, by December 8, the remnant was at Philadelphia in a state of great discouragement and demoralization. The Continental Congress, fearing capture, fled to Baltimore and, moved to

ENGLAND AND AMERICA 85

desperate measures, passed a resolution, giving Washington for six months unlimited authority to raise recruits, appoint and dismiss officers, impress provisions, and arrest loyalists. Howe felt that the rebellion was at an end. On November 30 he issued a proclamation offering pardon to all who would take the oath of allegiance within sixty days; and farmers in New Jersey took it by hundreds, securing in return a certificate of loyalty. The rebels' cause seemed lost. But at the moment when, if ever, it was worth while to push pursuit to the uttermost, with the prospect of reducing three colonies and breaking up all show of resistance, Howe, satisfied with his campaign, began to prepare winter quarters.

To the northward, a similar fatality seemed to prevent full British success. During the summer, General Guy Carleton waited at the northern end of Lake Champlain while his carpenters built gunboats. Month after month went by until, on October 11, the British vessels engaged Arnold's inferior flotilla. Two days of hot fighting with musketry and cannon resulted in the destruction of the American squadron, so that the way seemed clear for Carleton to advance; but the season was late, the difficulties of getting provisions from Canada seemed excessive, and on November 2 the British withdrew. Here again only extreme caution and slowness permitted the colonial army to hold its ground. Yet it seemed doubtful whether the American cause might not collapse even without further pressure, for the "armies" were almost gone by sheer disintegration. General Schuyler had a scanty 3,000 near Lake Champlain; Washington could not muster over 6,000 at Philadelphia, and these were on the points of going home. The attempt to carry on the war by voluntary militia fighting was a visible failure.

At this stage, the darkest hour, Washington, who had never dared to risk a battle, took the bold step of re-crossing the Delaware with part of his half-starved and shivering troops, and captured nearly all of a Hessian encampment at Trenton on December 25. Further, he drew on Cornwallis to advance against him, skirmished successfully on January 2, and then, moving by a night march to the British rear, defeated a regiment at Princeton. Cornwallis, with 7,000 men, was out-generalled by Washington in this affair, which was the first really aggressive blow struck by the Americans. The result was to lead Howe to abandon the effort to hold all of New Jersey; while Washington was able to post his men in winter quarters at Morristown, where he could watch every British move. This masterly little campaign, carried on under every disadvantage, made Washington's fame secure, and undoubtedly saved the American revolution from breaking down. It revived the fighting spirit, encouraged the Congress and the people, and created a faith in Washington on the part of the soldiers and farmers which was destined to grow steadily into love and veneration. With no particular military insight beyond common sense and the comprehension of military virtues, he was a man of iron will, extreme personal courage, and a patience and tenacity which had no limit.

Congress now showed that its members realized in part the military lesson, for it authorized a standing regular army, and gave Washington power to establish it and appoint lower officers. It was a hard task to induce any Americans to enlist in such an organization; but little by little there were collected " Continental troops " who did not rush back to their family duties at the end of three months, but stayed and grew in discipline and steadiness. Yet Washington could never count on more than a few thousand such; Americans in general simply would not fight except under pressure of invasion and in defence of their homes.

During 1776–7, the revolted communities assumed something of the appearance of settled governments. The States replaced their revolutionary conventions with constitutions closely modelled upon their provincial institutions, but with elective governors, and, to safeguard liberty, full control over legislation, taxation, and most offices placed in the hands of the legislatures. Executive power was confined mainly to military matters. The Continental Congress continued to act as a grand committee of safety, framing recommendations and requests to the States, and issuing paper money on the credit of its constituents. Military administration proved a task beyond the capacity of the new governments, even for such diminutive armies as those which guarded the northern frontier and New Jersey, and the forces suffered from lack of food, covering, and powder. The country had few sources of supplies and wretched roads.

In 1777, when spring opened, the British armies slowly prepared to push matters to a definite conclusion. The North Cabinet, especially Lord George Germaine, had no single coherent plan of operations beyond continuing the lines laid down in 1776. It was early planned to have the Canadian force march southward and join Howe, collecting supplies and gathering recruits as it traversed New York. Howe was told that he was expected to co-operate, but was not prevented from substituting a plan of his own which involved capturing Philadelphia, the chief American town and, as the seat of the Continental Congress, the "rebel capital." Germaine merely intimated that Howe ought to make such speedy work as to return in time to meet the Canadian force, but did not give him any positive order, so Howe considered his plan approved. In leisurely fashion he tried twice to march across New Jersey in June; but, although he had 17,000 to Washington's 8,000, he would not risk leaving the latter in his rear and withdrew. He next determined to move by water, and began the sea journey on July 5. This process occupied not less than six weeks, since he first tried to sail up the Delaware, only to withdraw from before the American forts; and it was not until August 22 that he finally landed his men at the head of Chesapeake Bay.

Meanwhile, General Burgoyne, a man of fashion as well as an officer, had begun his march southward from Lake Champlain with 7,500 men and some Indian allies, forced the Americans to evacuate Fort Ticonderoga without a blow, and chased the garrison to the southward and eastward. Pushing forward in spite of blocked roads and burned bridges, he reached the Hudson River on August 1 without mishap, and there halted to collect provisions and await reinforcements from Tories and from a converging expedition under St. Leger, which was to join him by way of Lake Ontario and the Mohawk Valley. Up to this time the American defence had been futile. It seemed as though nothing could stop Burgoyne's advance. Congress now appointed a new general, Gates, to whom Washington sent General Morgan with some of his best troops. While Burgoyne waited, the militia of New England began collecting, and presently, on August 15 and 16, two detachments of the British sent to seize stores at Bennington were surrounded and captured. St. Leger, unable to manage his Indian allies, or force the surrender of the American Fort Stanwix, was obliged, on August 22, to retreat. Burgoyne, with diminishing numbers and no hope of reinforcement, found himself confronted by rapidly growing swarms of enemies. At the moment when his need of co-operation from Howe became acute, the latter general was two hundred miles away in Pennsylvania.

Under the circumstances, the two campaigns worked themselves out to independent conclusions. In Pennsylvania, Washington boldly marched his summer army with its nucleous of veterans out to meet the British, and challenged a battle along the banks of the Brandywine creek. On September 11, Howe, with 18,000 men, methodically attacked

Washington, who had not over 11,000, sent a flanking column around his right wing, and after a stiff resistance pushed the Americans from the field. There was no pursuit; and four days later Washington was prevented only by bad weather from risking another fight. He did not feel able to prevent Howe from entering Philadelphia on September 27; but on October 3, taking advantage of a division of the British army, he assumed the offensive at Germantown and brought his unsteady forces into action, only to suffer another defeat. With this Washington was forced to abandon operations in the field and to go into winter quarters at Valley Forge, not far from the city; while Howe besieged and on November 2 took the American forts on the Delaware. The British campaign was successful; Philadelphia was theirs, and they had won every engagement. But nothing shows more clearly Washington's ability as a fighter and leader than his stubborn contest against odds in this summer.

Meanwhile, the Northern campaign came to its conclusion. By September, Gates, the new commander, found himself at the head of nearly 20,000 men, and Burgoyne's case grew desperate. He made two efforts to break through to the southward, at Freeman's Farm, and again at Bemis Heights, but was met by superior numbers and overwhelmed, in spite of the gallantry of his troops. Forced back to Saratoga on the Hudson River, he was surrounded and at length compelled to surrender, on October 17. Sir Henry Clinton, who commanded the British garrison of New York in Howe's absence, sent a small expedition up the Hudson; but it did not penetrate nearer than sixty miles from the spot where Burgoyne stood at bay, and it achieved nothing more than a raid. So the northern British force, sent to perform an impossible task, was destroyed solely because neither Howe nor his superiors realized the necessity of providing for certain co-operation from the southward. The prisoners, according to the terms of the surrender, were to be returned to England; but Congress, owing in part to some complaints of Burgoyne, chose to violate the agreement, and the captive British and Hessians were retained. Burgoyne himself returned to England, burning with anger against Howe and the North Ministry.

The winter of 1777–8 found the two British armies comfortably housed in New York and Philadelphia, and Washington, with his handful of miserably equipped men, presenting the skeleton of an army at Valley Forge. Congress, now manned by less able leaders than at first, was almost won over to displacing the unsuccessful commander by Gates, the victor of Saratoga; and it did go so far as to commit the administration of the army to a cabal of Gates's friends, who carried on a campaign of depreciation and backbiting against Washington. But the whole unworthy plot broke down under a few vigorous words from the latter, the would-be rival quailing before the Virginian's personal authority. He was not a safe man to bait. The military headship remained securely with the one general capable of holding things together.

In the winter of 1778, however, a new element entered the game, namely, the possibility of French intervention. From the outbreak of the Revolution, very many Americans saw that their former deadly enemy, France, would be likely to prove an ally against England; and as early as 1776 American emissaries began to sound the court of Versailles. In March, 1776, Silas Deane was regularly commissioned by the Continental Congress, and in the autumn he was followed by no less a person than Benjamin Franklin. It was the duty of these men to get whatever aid they could, especially to seek an alliance. The young king, Louis XVI, was not a man of any independent statecraft; but his ministers, above all Vergennes, in charge of foreign affairs, were anxious to secure revenge upon England for the damage done by Pitt, and the tone of the French court was emphatically warlike. The financial weakness of the French government, destined shortly to pave the way for the Revolution, was clearly visible to Turgot, the Minister of Finances, and he with a few others protested against the expense of a foreign war; but Vergennes carried the day.

As early as the summer of 1776, French arms and munitions were being secretly supplied, while the Foreign Minister solemnly assured the watchful Lord Stormont, the English Ambassador, of his government's perfect neutrality. Thousands of muskets, hundreds of cannon, and quantities of clothes were thus shipped, and sums of money were also turned over to Franklin. Beaumarchais, the playwright and adventurer, acted with gusto the part of intermediary; and the lords and ladies of the French court, amusing themselves with " philosophy " and speculative liberalism, made a pet of the witty and sagacious Franklin. His popularity actually rivalled that of Voltaire when the latter, in 1778, returned to see Paris and die. But not until the colonies had proved that they could meet the English in battle with some prospect of success would the French commit themselves openly; and during 1776 and 1777 the tide ran too steadily against

ENGLAND AND AMERICA

the insurgents. Finally, in December, when the anxieties of Franklin and his associates were almost unendurable, the news of Burgoyne's surrender was brought to Paris. The turning-point was reached. Vergennes immediately led the French King to make two treaties, one for commercial reciprocity, the other a treaty of military alliance, recognizing the independence of the United States, and pledging the countries to make no separate peace. In the spring of 1778 the news reached America; and the war now entered upon a second stage.

There can be little doubt that under abler commanders the British armies might have crushed out all armed resistance in the middle colonies. In spite of all drawbacks, the trained British soldiers and officers were so superior in the field to the American levies on every occasion where the forces were not overwhelmingly unequal that it is impossible for any but the most bigoted American partisan to deny this possibility. Had there been a blockade, so that French and Dutch goods would have been excluded; had General Howe possessed the faintest spark of energy in following up his successes; had the North Cabinet not failed to compel Howe to co-operate with Burgoyne, the condition of things in 1778 might well have been so serious for the colonists' cause that Vergennes would have felt a French intervention to be fruitless. In that case, it is hard to see how the rebellion could have failed to be crushed in the next year. As it was, the Americans, by luck and by the tenacity of Washington and a few other leaders, had won the first victory.

CHAPTER V

FRENCH INTERVENTION AND BRITISH FAILURE, 1778–1781

DURING the two years of fighting, the party situation in England had grown increasingly bitter. The Whigs, joined now by young Charles Fox, unremittingly denounced the war as a crime, sympathized with the rebels, and execrated the cruelty of the Ministers while deriding their abilities. Parliament rang with vituperation; personal insults flew back and forth. From time to time Chatham took part in the attack, joining Burke and Fox in an opposition never surpassed for oratorical power. But the Ministerial party, secure in its strength, pushed on its way. The King now regarded the war as the issue

ENGLAND AND AMERICA

upon which he had staked his personal honour, and would tolerate no faltering. Yet in the winter of 1778 the rumours of a French alliance thickened; and, when the probability seemed to be a certainty, North made a desperate effort to end the war through a policy of granting everything except independence. In a speech of incredible assurance, he observed that he had never favoured trying to tax America, and brought in a Bill by which every parliamentary measure complained of by the Americans was repealed, and the right of internal taxation was expressly renounced. Amid the dejection of the Tories and the sneers of the Whigs, this measure became law, March 2, 1778; and commissioners, empowered to grant general amnesty, were sent with it to the United States.

At no other time in English history would it have been possible for a Ministry thus utterly to reverse its policy and remain in office; but North's tenure depended on influences outside the House of Commons, and he continued in his place. So severe was the crisis that an effort was made to arrange a coalition Ministry, with the aged Chatham at its head; George III, however, positively refused to permit North to surrender the first place. He would consent to Whigs entering the Cabinet only in subordinate positions. This obstinacy and the sudden death of Chatham blocked all coalition proposals, and left the war to continue as a party measure, not national in its character—the " King's war."

In America, the task of the commissioners proved hopeless. The men now in control of the Continental Congress and the State governments were pledged to independence from the bottom of their souls; and in the course of months of appeals, and attempts at negotiations, the commissioners failed to secure even a hearing. Congress ratified the French treaties with enthusiasm. That their proposal if made before the Declaration would have been successful can scarcely be doubted. It might even have produced an effect after 1776 had it been made by a Whig Ministry, headed by Chatham. But coming in 1778, after three years of war, when every vestige of the former sentiment of loyalty was dead, and offered by the same North Ministry which had brought on the revolution, it was foredoomed to defeat.

The war now entered upon a second phase, in which England found itself harder pressed than at any time in its history. It had not an ally in the world, and could count on no Rhine campaigns to exhaust French resources. For the first time England engaged France in a purely naval war; and for the only time France was sufficiently strong in sail-of-the-line to meet England on equal terms. The French fleet, rebuilt since 1763, was in excellent condition; the British navy, on the contrary, under the slack administration of Lord Sandwich, was worse off in equipment, repairs, number of sailors, and *esprit de corps* than at any time in the century. The French were able to send fleets unhindered wherever they wished; and when Spain entered as an ally, in 1779, their combined navies swept the Channel, driving the humiliated British fleet into port. England was called upon to make defensive war at home, at Gibraltar, in the West Indies, and finally in India, at a time when the full strength of the country was already occupied with the rebellion.

This led to an alteration of military methods in America. The policy of moving heavy armies was abandoned; and the British, forced to withdraw troops to garrison the West Indies and Florida, began the practice of wearing down the revolted colonies by raids and destruction of property. George III especially approved this punitive policy. As a first step, the army in Philadelphia marched back to New York, attacked on its retreat by Washington at Monmouth on June 27, 1778. The American advance was badly handled by General Lee, and fell back before the British; but Washington in person rallied his men, resumed the attack, and held his position.

Clinton, who succeeded Howe, continued his march, and the British army now settled down in New York, not to depart from its safe protection except on raids.

Washington accordingly posted his forces, as in 1777, outside the city, and awaited events. He could assume the offensive only in case a French fleet should assist him, and this happened but twice, in 1778, and not again for three years. The first time, Admiral D'Estaing with a strong fleet menaced New York and then Newport, the latter in conjunction with an American land force. But before each port he was foiled by the superior skill of Admiral Howe; and he finally withdrew without risking a battle, to the intense disgust of the Americans. For the rest, the war in the northern States dwindled to raids by the British along the Connecticut coast and into New Jersey, and outpost affairs on the Hudson, in some of which Washington's Continental troops showed real brilliancy in attack. But with the British in command of the sea little could be done to meet the raids, and southern Connecticut was ravaged with fire and sword.

At the same time, the States suffered the horrors of Indian war, since the Tories and British from Canada utilized the Iroquois and the Ohio Valley Indians as allies. The New York frontier was in continual distress;

ENGLAND AND AMERICA 101

and the Pennsylvania and Maryland and Virginia settlements felt the scalping knife and torch. Hamilton, the British commander at the post of Detroit, paid a fixed price for scalps, and was known as "the hair buyer." Against the Iroquois, Sullivan led an expedition in 1779 which could not bring the savages to a decisive battle, although he ravaged their lands and crippled their resources. Against the north-western Indians, a daring Virginian, George Rogers Clark, led a counter-raid which captured several posts in the territory north of the Ohio River, and finally took Hamilton himself prisoner at Vincennes. In every such war the sufferings of the settlers outnumbered a hundred-fold all that they could inflict in return, and this consciousness burned into their souls a lasting hatred of England, the ally of the murdering, torturing devils from the forests.

While the British fleets fought indecisive actions in European waters, or near the West Indies, the British raiding policy was transferred to a new region, namely, the southern States, which thus far had known little of the severities of war. In December, 1778, an expedition under Prevost easily occupied Savannah, driving the Georgia militia away. The next year an effort was made by an American force, in combination with the French fleet under D'Estaing, who returned from the West Indies, to recapture the place. The siege was formed, and there appeared some prospects of a successful outcome, but the French admiral, too restless to wait until the completion of siege operations, insisted on trying to take the city by storm on October 9. The result was a complete repulse, after which D'Estaing sailed away, and the American besiegers were obliged to withdraw. The real interests of the French were, in fact, in the West Indies, where they were gradually capturing English islands; their contributions so far to the American cause consisted in gifts of munitions and loans of money, together with numerous adventurous officers who aspired to lead the American armies. The most amiable and attractive of these was the young Marquis de Lafayette, owing largely to whose influence a force of French soldiers under de Rochambeau was sent in 1780 to America. But for months this force was able to do no more than remain in camp at Newport, Rhode Island, blockaded by the English fleet.

In 1780, the British raiding policy was resumed in the southern States and achieved a startling success. In January, Clinton sailed from New York with a force of 8,000 men, and after driving the American levies into the city of Charleston, South Carolina, besieged and took it on May 12, with all its defenders. He then returned to New York, leaving Lord Cornwallis with a few troops to complete the conquest of the State. Congress now sent General Gates southward to repeat the triumph of Saratoga. At Camden, on August 16, 1780, the issue was decided. The American commander, with only 3,000 men, encountered Cornwallis, who had about 2,200, and, as usual, the militia, when attacked by British in the open field, fled for their lives at the first charge of the redcoats, leaving the few continentals to be outnumbered and crushed.

For a period of several weeks all organized American resistance disappeared. Only bands of guerillas, or "partisans," as they were called, kept the field. Clinton had issued a proclamation calling all loyalists to join the ranks; and Cornwallis made a systematic effort to compel the enrolment of Tory militia. The plan bore fruit in an apparent large increase of British numbers, but also in the outbreak of a murderous civil war. Raiding parties on both sides took to ambuscades, nocturnal house-burning, hanging of prisoners, and downright massacres. Pre-eminent for his success was the British Colonel Tarleton, who with a body of light troops swept tirelessly around, breaking up rebel bands, riding down militia, and rendering his command a terror to the

State. Marion, Sumter, and other Americans struggled vainly to equal his exploits.

Occasional American successes could not turn back the tide. On October 18, 1780, a band of Tories under General Ferguson ventured too far to the westward, and at King's Mountain were surrounded and shot or taken prisoners by a general uprising of the frontiersmen. General Greene, who replaced Gates in December, managed to rally a few men, but dared not meet Cornwallis in the field. His lieutenant, Morgan, when pursued by Tarleton, turned on him at the Cowpens, and on January 17 managed to inflict a severe defeat. The forces were diminutive—less than a thousand on each side—but the battle was skilfully fought. After it, however, both Morgan and Greene were forced to fly northward, and did not escape Cornwallis's pursuit until they were driven out of North Carolina. The State seemed lost, and on February 23, Cornwallis issued a proclamation calling upon all loyalists to join the royal forces. Meanwhile, encouraged by the striking successes in the Carolinas, Clinton sent a force under Arnold to Virginia, which marched unopposed through the seaboard counties of that State in the winter of 1781. It seemed as though the new British policy were on the verge of a great triumph.

By this time it was becoming a grave question whether the American revolution was not going to collapse from sheer weakness. The confederation, as a general government, seemed to be on the verge of breaking down. The State governments, although badly hampered wherever British raids took place, were operating regularly and steadily, but the only common government continued to be the voluntary Continental Congress, whose powers were entirely undefined, and rested, in fact, on sufferance. In 1776 a committee, headed by John Dickinson, drafted Articles of Confederation which, if adopted promptly, would have provided a regular form of government; but, although these were submitted in 1777 for ratification, inter-state jealousy sufficed to block their acceptance. It was discovered that all those States which, by their original charters, were given no definite western boundaries, were disposed to claim an extension of their territory to the Mississippi River. Virginia, through her general, Clark, actually occupied part of the region claimed by her, and assumed to grant lands there. The representatives of Maryland in Congress declared such inequality a danger to the union, and refused to sign the Articles unless the land claims west of the mountains were surrendered to the general government.

This determination was formally approved by the Maryland legislature in February, 1779, and matters remained at a standstill. At last, in 1780, Congress offered to hold any lands which might be granted to it, with the pledge to form them into States, and, following this, New York, and Virginia intimated a willingness to make the required cessions. Then Maryland yielded and ratified the Articles, so that they came into operation on March 2, 1781.

The self-styled " United States " had now travelled so far on the road to bankruptcy that the adoption of the " Articles of Perpetual Union " seemed scarcely more than an empty form. In the first place, the federal finances were prostrate. The device of issuing paper money had proved fatal, for, after a brief period, in 1775, the excessive issues depreciated in spite of every effort to hinder their decline by proclamations, price conventions, and political pressure. The only way of sustaining such notes, namely, the furnishing by the States of a full and sufficient revenue, was never attempted; for the States themselves preferred to issue notes, rather than to tax, and when called upon by the Continental Congress for requisitions they turned over such amounts of paper as they saw fit. By 1780, the " continental currency " was practically worthless. Congress could rely only upon such small sums of money as it could raise by foreign loans through Franklin and by the contributions of a few patriotic people, notably Robert Morris.

The maintenance of the army exhausted the resources of Congress, and every winter saw the story of Valley Forge repeated. To secure supplies, Congress was driven to authorize seizure and impressment of food and payment in certificates of indebtedness. It was for this reason, as well as from the unwillingness of the Americans to enlist for the war, that the Continental forces dwindled to diminutive numbers in 1781. Nothing but Washington's tireless tenacity and loyalty held the army together, and kept the officers from resigning in disgust. Yet it seemed impossible that Washington himself could carry the burden much longer. The general government appeared to be on the point of disintegrating, leaving to the separate States the task of defending themselves. Everywhere lassitude, preoccupation with local matters, a disposition to leave the war to the French, a willingness to let other States bear the burdens, replaced the fervour of 1776. In other words, the old colonial habits were reasserting themselves, and the separate States, reverting to their former accustomed negative politics, were behaving toward the Continental Congress precisely as they had done toward England itself during the French wars. With hundreds of thousands of men of fighting age in America it was impossible, in 1781, to collect more than a handful for service away from their homes. The essentially unmilitary nature of the Americans was not to be changed.

Fortunately for the rebels, the policy of Great Britain was such as to give them a lease of hope. In spite of the great British naval power during the first two years of the war, no blockade had been attempted; and after 1778 the British fleets were thoroughly occupied in following and foiling the French. The result was that commerce of a sort continued throughout the war, armed privateers and merchantmen venturing from the New England and other ports, and trading with France, Spain and the West Indies. Hundreds were taken by British cruisers, but hundreds more continued their dangerous trade, and so America continued to receive imports. The Dutch, especially, supplied the revolted colonies with some of the commodities which their exclusion from British ports rendered scarce. So, except for paper money, there was no economic distress.

In 1781, when if ever the British might hope to reduce the colonies, the Empire was itself in sore straits for men to fill its ships and garrison its forts. This made it difficult for England to send any reinforcements to America, and left Clinton and Cornwallis with about 27,000 men to complete their raiding campaign. The task proved excessive. In March, 1781, Greene, having assembled a small force, gave battle to Cornwallis at Guilford Court House. The little army of British veterans, only 2,219 in all, drove Greene from the field after a stiff fight, but were so reduced in numbers that Cornwallis felt obliged to retreat to Wilmington on the coast, where he was entirely out of the field of campaign. On April 25 he marched northward into Virginia to join the force which had been there for several months, took command, and continued the policy of marching and destroying. Before his arrival, Washington had tried to use the French force at Newport against the Virginia raiders; but the French squadron, although it ventured from port in March, 1781, and had a successful encounter with a British fleet, declined to push on into the Chesapeake, and the plan was abandoned. Cornwallis was able to march unhindered by any French danger during the summer of 1781.

But while the British were terrifying Virginia and chasing militia, the forces left in the Carolinas were being worn down by

Greene and his " partisan " allies. On April 25, at Hobkirk's Hill, Rawdon, the British commander defeated Greene, and then, with reduced ranks, retreated. During the summer, further sieges and raids recaptured British posts, and on September 8 another battle took place at Eutaw Springs. This resulted, as usual, in a British success on the battlefield and a retreat afterwards. By October, the slender British forces in the southernmost States were cooped up in Charleston and Savannah, and a war of extermination was stamping out all organized Tory resistance. The raiding policy had failed through weakness of numbers. The superior fighting ability and tactical skill of Cornwallis, Rawdon, Stuart, and Tarleton were as obvious as the courage and steadiness of their troops; but their means were pitifully inadequate to the task assigned them.

Further north, a still greater failure took place. Washington was not deterred by the futile outcome of his previous attempts to use French co-operation from making a patient and urgent effort to induce De Grasse, the French admiral in the West Indies, to come north and join with him and Rochambeau in an attack on Cornwallis in Virginia. He was at last successful; and on August 28 the wished-for fleet, a powerful collection of twenty-eight sail-of-the-line, with frigates, reached Chesapeake Bay. Already the French troops from Newport, and part of the American army from outside New York, had begun their southward march, carefully concealing their purposes from Clinton, and were moving through Pennsylvania. As a third part of the combination, the French squadron from Newport put to sea, bringing eight more sail-of-the-line, which, added to De Grasse's, would overmatch any British fleet on the western side of the Atlantic.

The one disturbing possibility was that the British West India fleet, which very properly had sailed in pursuit, might defeat the two French fleets singly. This chance was put to the test on September 5. On that day Admiral Graves, with nineteen men-of-war, attacked De Grasse, who brought twenty-four into line outside Chesapeake Bay; and the decisive action of the Revolution took place. Seldom has a greater stake been played for by a British fleet, and seldom has a naval battle been less successfully managed. Graves may have intended to concentrate upon part of the French line, but his subordinates certainly failed to understand any such purpose; and the outcome was that the head of the British column, approaching the French line at an angle, was severely handled, while the rear took no part in the battle. The fleets separated without decisive result, and the British, after cruising a few days irresolutely, gave up and returned to New York. The other French squadron had meanwhile arrived, and the allied troops had come down the Chesapeake. Cornwallis, shut up in Yorktown by overwhelming forces, defended himself until October 17, and then surrendered with 8,000 men to the man who had beaten him years before at Trenton and Princeton. Clinton, aware at last of his danger, sailed with every vessel he could scrape together, and approached the bay on October 24 with twenty-five sail-of-the-line and 7,000 men; but it was too late. He could only retreat to New York, where he remained in the sole British foothold north of Charleston and Savannah.

Washington would have been glad to retain De Grasse and undertake further combined manœuvres; but the French admiral was anxious to return to the West Indies, and so the military operations of the year ended. More was in reality unnecessary, for the collapse of the British military policy was manifest, and the surrender of Cornwallis was a sufficiently striking event to bring the war to a close. Washington had not won the last fight with his own Continentals. The co-operation not only of the French fleet but of the French troops under Rochambeau had played the decisive part. Yet it was his planning, his tenacity, his personal authority with French and Americans that determined the combined operation and made it successful. In the midst of a half-starved, ill-equipped army, a disintegrating, bankrupt government, and a people whose fighting spirit was rapidly dwindling, it was he with his officers who had saved the Revolution at the last gasp.

It was no less the British mismanagement which made this possible, for had not Howe, by delays, thrown away his chances; had not Howe and Burgoyne and Clinton and Cornwallis, by their failures to co-operate, made it possible for their armies to be taken separately; had not the navy omitted to apply a blockade; had not the Ministry, in prescribing a raiding policy, failed to strain every nerve to furnish an adequate supply of men, the outcome would have been different. As it was, the British defeat could no longer be concealed by the end of 1781. The attempt to conquer America had failed.

CHAPTER VI

BRITISH PARTIES AND AMERICAN
INDEPENDENCE, 1778–1783

WHEN the news of the surrender of Cornwallis at Yorktown reached England, it was recognized by Whigs and Tories alike that the time had come to admit the failure of the war. The loss of 7,000 troops was not in itself a severe blow, at a time when England had over 200,000 men under arms in various parts of the world; but it actually marked the breakdown of the American campaign, and, what was still more significant, the political bankruptcy of the North Ministry. Ever since 1778, the tide had been rising against the royal policy. At first, when the French war began, the nation rallied against the ancient foe and there was some enthusiasm displayed in recruiting and furnishing supplies; but, as general after general returned from America—first Burgoyne, then Howe and his brother, the admiral,—to rise in Parliament and denounce the administrative incompetence which had foiled their efforts; as month after month passed and no victory either in America or Europe came to cheer the public; worst of all, when, in 1779, and again in 1780, combined French and Spanish fleets swept the Channel

ENGLAND AND AMERICA 115

in overpowering numbers, driving the English fleet into Torbay harbour—the war spirit dwindled, and bitter criticism took its place.

The Whig Opposition, no longer hampered by having the defence of the revolted colonists as their sole issue, denounced in unmeasured language the incompetence, corruption, and despotism of the North Ministry, singling out Sandwich, at the Admiralty, and Germaine, Secretary for the Colonies, as objects for especial invective. Party hatred festered in army and navy, Whig and Tory admirals distrusting each other and engaging in bitter quarrels, Whig and Tory generals criticizing one another's plans and motives. On his part, Lord North felt, as early as 1779, that his task was hopeless, and sought repeatedly to resign; but in spite of secessions from the Ministry, in spite of defeats and humiliations such as the control by the allies of the Channel, nothing could shake George's determination. He would never consent to abandon the colonies or permit North to surrender to the detested Whigs.

In 1780, the Opposition, led by Fox and Burke, began to direct its fire at the King himself; and finally, in March of that year, they had the satisfaction of carrying in the Commons, by votes of men who once had been on the administration side, a resolution to the effect that " the power of the Crown has increased, is increasing, and ought to be diminished." This was carried, by 233 votes to 215, in a House where four years before the total Opposition mustered only a hundred. Measures to cut down sinecures, to limit the secret service fund, to take away opportunities for royal corruption, were introduced by Burke and, although defeated, drew large votes.

The tenacious politician who wore the crown was not yet beaten. In the summer of 1780, the disgraceful Gordon riots broke out in London; and the King, by his courageous personal bearing and bold direction of affairs, won momentary prestige. The news from America, moreover, was brighter than for a long time, and the British defence of Gibraltar was unshaken. Suddenly dissolving Parliament, the King employed every resource of influence or pressure, and managed to secure once more a majority in the House of Commons. During the year 1781, the North Ministry breathed more freely, and was able to repel Whig attacks by safe majorities. But the respite was short.

In the winter session of 1782, the news of Yorktown shook the Ministry to its centre, and on top of that came the reports of the surrender of Minorca, St. Kitts, and Nevis. Held together only by the inflexible determination of George III never to yield American independence or "stoop to opposition," the Ministers fought bitterly though despairingly against a succession of Whig motions, censuring the Admiralty, demanding the withdrawal of the troops, and finally censuring the Ministry. Majorities dwindled as rats began to leave the sinking ship. On March 8, North escaped censure by ten votes only. The King made repeated efforts to induce members of the Opposition to come into some sort of coalition, but the hatred was too fierce, the divergence of principle too wide. Rockingham would accept only absolute surrender. On March 15, a resolution of want of confidence was lost by nine only.

Five days later, in face of a renewed motion of the same kind, North announced his resignation. The end had come. The system of George III had broken down, ruined by the weaknesses of the Tory Cabinet in administration, in war, and in diplomacy, the most disastrous Ministry in the history of England. There was no possible doubt as to the significance of the collapse, for Lord Rockingham took office with a Whig Cabinet, containing Shelburne and Fox, steadfast friends of America, as Secretaries of State, and with the avowed purpose of conceding independence to the former colonies, while maintaining the contest with Spain and France.

THE WARS BETWEEN

Interest now shifted from the battlefield to the regions of diplomacy, where the situation was complicated and delicate, owing to the unusual relations of the parties involved. The United States and France were in alliance, each pledged not to make a separate peace. Spain was in alliance with France for the purpose of recovering Gibraltar, Minorca, and Florida, but was not in any alliance with the United States. The French government, tied thus to two allies, recognized the possible contingency of diverging interests between Spain and the United States, and exerted all the influence it could to keep diplomatic control in its own hands. This it accomplished through its representatives in America, especially de la Luzerne, who wielded an immense prestige with the members of the Continental Congress, not only through his position as representative of the power whose military, naval, and financial aid was absolutely indispensable, but also by means of personal intrigues of a type hitherto more familiar in European courts than in simple America. Under his direction, Congress authorized its European representatives, Franklin, Jay, and Adams, accredited to France, Spain, and the Netherlands respectively, to act as peace commissioners and to be guided in all things by the advice and consent of the French Minister,

ENGLAND AND AMERICA 119

Vergennes. Their instructions designated boundaries, indemnity for ravages and for the taking of slaves, and a possible cession of Canada, but all were made subject to French approval. When, accordingly, in 1781, both Shelburne and Fox of the Rockingham Ministry sought to open negotiations with the American representatives, while pushing on vigorously the war against France and Spain, they interjected an embarrassing element into the situation. Vergennes could not prohibit American negotiation, but he relied upon the instructions of the commissioners to enable him to prevent the making of any separate peace, contrary to the treaty of 1778.

The first steps were taken by Franklin and Shelburne, who opened unofficial negotiations through Richard Oswald, a friend of America. It seems to have been Shelburne's plan to avoid the preliminary concession of independence, hoping to retain some form of connection between America and England, or at least to use independence as a make-weight in the negotiations. Hence Oswald, his agent, was not commissioned to deal with the United States as such. Fox, Secretary for Foreign Affairs, felt, on the other hand, that the negotiation belonged to his field, and he sent Thomas Grenville to Paris, authorized to deal with France and, indirectly, with the United States. Over this difference in the Cabinet, and over other matters, an acute personal rivalry developed between Fox and Shelburne, which culminated when Rockingham died in July, 1782. George III, who much preferred Shelburne to Fox, asked him to form a Ministry, and upon his acceptance Fox, absolutely refusing to serve under him, withdrew from the Cabinet, carrying his friends with him. Thus the triumphant Whig party was split within a few months after its victory. The whole responsibility now rested on Shelburne.

Meanwhile, a new situation had developed in Paris, for Jay and Adams, the other two commissioners, had brought about a change in the American policy. Franklin, deeply indebted to the French court and on the best of terms with Vergennes, was willing to credit him with good intentions and was ready to accept his advice to negotiate with England under the vague terms of Oswald's commission; but Jay, who had had a mortifying experience in Spain, suspected treachery and insisted that England must, in opening negotiations, fully recognize American independence. He was sure that Spain would gladly see the United States shut in to the Atlantic coast away from Spanish territory, and he felt certain that Vergennes was under Spanish influence. Adams, who knew nothing of Spain, but distrusted the French on general principles, sided with Jay; and Franklin, submitting to his colleagues, agreed to a curious diplomatic manœuvre. Jay sent to Shelburne a secret message, urging him to deal separately with the United States under a proper commission and not seek to play into the hands of Spain and France. He knew that a French emissary had visited Shelburne, and he dreaded French double-dealing, especially on the question of boundaries and fishery rights.

The British Prime Minister was in the odd position of being appealed to by one of the three hostile powers to save it from the other two; but underlying the situation was the fact that Shelburne, as a Whig since the beginning of the American quarrel, was committed to a friendly policy toward America. He knew, moreover, that when Parliament should meet he must expect trouble from Fox and the dissatisfied Whigs, as well as the Tories, and he was anxious to secure a treaty as soon as possible. So yielding, on September 27, he gave Oswald the required commission, but, suspecting that he was rather too complaisant, sent Henry Strachey to assist him. During the summer, Franklin and Oswald, in informal discussions, had already eliminated various matters, so that when negotiations formally opened it took not over five weeks to agree upon a draft treaty.

During all this time the Americans violated their instructions by failing to consult Vergennes. Here Franklin was again overruled by Jay and Adams, whose antipathy to French and Spanish influence was insuperable. It does not appear that Vergennes had any definite intention to work against American boundaries or fishery rights; but there can be no doubt that Rayneval and Marbois, two of his agents, committed themselves openly in a sense unfavourable to American claims, and it is likely that, had the negotiations taken place under his control, the outcome would have been delayed in every way in order to allow France to keep its contract with Spain, whose attacks on Gibraltar were pushed all through the summer. As it was, the negotiators managed to agree on a treaty of peace which reflected the Whig principles of Shelburne and the skill and pertinacity of the three Americans. Little trouble was encountered over boundaries, Shelburne ceding everything east of the Mississippi and north of Florida, and designating as a boundary between the United States and Canada in part the same line as that in the Proclamation of 1763, from the

St. Croix River to the eastward of Maine, to the Great Lakes and thence westward by a system of waterways to the headwaters of the Mississippi. At the especial urgence of Adams, whose Massachusetts constituents drew much of their wealth from the Newfoundland fisheries, the right of continuing this pursuit was comprised in the treaty, together with the right to land and dry fish on unoccupied territories in Labrador and Nova Scotia. As a possible makeweight, the navigation of the Mississippi was guaranteed to citizens of both the United States and Great Britain.

The chief difficulty arose over the question of the treatment of American loyalists and the payment of British debts which had been confiscated in every colony. Shelburne insisted that there must be restoration of civil rights, compensation for damages, and a pledge against any future confiscations or disfranchisements for loyalists, and also demanded a provision for the payment of all debts due to British creditors. Here the negotiation hung in a long deadlock, for Franklin, Adams, and Jay were unanimously determined to concede no compensation for individuals whom they hated as traitors; while the British negotiators felt bound in honour not to abandon the men who had lost all and suffered every indignity and humiliation as a penalty for their loyalty. At length, progress was made when Adams suggested that the question of British debts be separated from that of Tory compensation; so a clause was agreed upon guaranteeing the full payment of *bona fide* debts heretofore contracted.

Finally, after Franklin had raised a counter-claim for damages due to what he called the "inhuman burnings" of the British raids since 1778, it was agreed to insert a clause against any future confiscations or prosecutions of loyalists and to add that Congress should "earnestly recommend" to the States the restoration of loyalists' estates and the repealing of all laws against them. At the time the commissioners drew up this article, they must have known that the Congress of the United States had no power to enforce the treaty, and that any such recommendations, however "earnest," would carry no weight with the thirteen communities controlled by embittered rebels, who remembered every Tory, alive or dead, with execration. Nevertheless, it offered a way of escape, and the British representative signed, on November 30, 1782. The great contest was at an end.

When Franklin revealed to Vergennes that, unknown to the French court, the American commissioners had agreed on a draft treaty, the French minister was somewhat indignant at the trick, and communicated his displeasure to his agent in America. This induced the easily worried Congress to instruct Livingston, the Secretary for Foreign Affairs, to write a letter censuring the commissioners; but, although Jay and Adams were hotly indignant at such servility, the matter ended then and there. Vergennes's displeasure was momentary, and the French policy continued as before. The European war was, in fact, wearing to its end. Already, in April, 1782, Admiral Rodney had inflicted a sharp defeat on De Grasse, capturing five of his vessels, including the flagship with the admiral himself. This, together with the extreme inefficiency of the Spanish fleet, put an end to the hope of further French gains in the West Indies. Before Gibraltar, also, the allied fleet of forty-eight vessels did not dare to risk a general engagement with a British relieving fleet of thirty, and when in September, 1782, a final bombardment was attempted, the batteries from the fort proved too strong for their assailants. The allies felt that they had accomplished all they could hope to, and agreed to terms of peace on January 20, 1783. France gained little beyond sundry West India Islands, but Spain profited to the extent of regaining Minorca and also Florida. It was at best a defeat for England, and the Whig Ministry, which carried it through, was unable to prevent such an outcome.

The American peace was made the pretext for Shelburne's fall, since a coalition of dissatisfied Whigs and Tories united in March, 1783, to censure it, thereby turning out the Ministry. But, although Fox regained control of diplomatic matters and made some slight moves toward reopening negotiations, he had no serious intention of disturbing Shelburne's work, and the provisional treaty was made definitive on September 3, 1783—the day on which the French treaty was signed. Thus the Americans technically kept to the terms of their alliance with France in agreeing not to make a separate peace, but as a matter of fact hostilities had entirely ceased in America since January, 1783, and practically since the fall of the North Ministry. The British had remained quietly in New York and Charleston, withdrawing from all other points, and Washington with his small army stood at Newburg-on-the-Hudson. In October, 1783, the last British withdrew, taking with them into exile thousands of Tories who did not dare to remain to test the value of the clauses in the treaty of peace intended to protect them. So the last traces of the long contest disappeared, and the United States entered upon its career.

The treaty, as must have been foreseen by the commissioners themselves, remained a dead letter so far as the Tories were concerned. Congress performed its part and gave the promised recommendation, but the States paid no heed. The loyalists were not restored to civil or property rights. The plain provision of the treaty prohibiting further legislation against loyalists was defied in several States, and additional disqualifications were placed upon those who dared to remain in the country. The provision regarding the payment of debts remained unfulfilled, since there was no mechanism provided in the treaty through which the article could be enforced. Only from the British government could the Tories receive any recompense for their sufferings, and there they were in part relieved. Very many received grants of land in Canada, where they formed a considerable part of the population in several districts. More went to New Brunswick and Nova Scotia to receive similar grants. Others spent their days in England as unhappy pensioners, forgotten victims of a war which all Englishmen sought to bury in oblivion. Those who remained in the United States ultimately regained standing and fared better than the exiles, but not until new domestic issues had arisen to obliterate the memory of revolutionary antagonisms.

With the Treaty of 1782, the mother country and the former colonies definitely started on separate paths, recognizing the fundamental differences which for fifty years had made harmonious co-operation impossible. England remained as before, aristocratic in social structure, oligarchic in government, military and naval in temper—a land of strongly fixed standards of religious and political life, a country where society looked to a narrow circle for leadership. Its commercial and economic ideals, unaltered by defeat, persisted to guide national policy in peace and war for two more generations. The sole result of the war for England was to render impossible in future any such perversion of Cabinet government as that which George III, by intimidation, fraud, and political management, had succeeded for a decade in establishing. Never again would the country tolerate royal dictation of policies and leaders. England became what it had been before 1770, a country where parliamentary groups and leaders bore the responsibility and gained the glory or discredit, while the outside public approved or protested without seeking in any other manner to control the destinies of the State. While the English thus sullenly fell back into their accustomed habits, the former Colonies, now relieved from the old-time subordination, were turned adrift to solve problems of a wholly different sort.

CHAPTER VII

THE FORMATION OF THE UNITED STATES, 1781–1793

THE British colonists, who assumed independent legal existence with the adoption of Articles of Confederation in 1781, had managed to carry through a revolution and emerge into the light of peace. They were now required to learn, in the hard school of experience, those necessary facts of government which they had hitherto ignored, and which, even in the agonies of civil war, they had refused to recognize.

Probably with three-quarters of the American people, the prevailing political sentiment was that of aversion to any governmental control, coupled with a deep-rooted jealousy and distrust of all officials, even those chosen by and dependent upon themselves. Their political ideals contemplated the government of each colony chiefly by the elected representatives of the voters, who should meet annually to legislate and tax, and then, having defined the duties of the few permanent officers in such a way as to leave them little or no discretion, should dissolve, leaving the community to run itself until the next annual session. Authority of any kind was to them an object of traditional dread, even when exercised by their own agents. The early State constitutions concentrated all power in the legislature, leaving the executive and judicial officials little to do but execute the laws. The only discretionary powers enjoyed by governors were in connection with military affairs.

In establishing the Articles of Confederation the statesmen of the Continental Congress had no intention of creating in any sense a governing body. All that the Congress could do was to decide upon war and peace, make treaties, decide upon a common military establishment, and determine the sums to be contributed to the common treasury. These matters, moreover, called for an affirmative vote of nine States in each case. There was no federal executive or judiciary, nor any provision for enforcing the votes of the Congress. To carry out any single thing committed by the Articles to the Congress, and duly voted, required the posi-

ENGLAND AND AMERICA 131

tive co-operation of the State legislatures, who were under no other compulsion than their sense of what the situation called for and of what they could afford to do.

Things were, in short, just where the colonists would have been glad to have them before the Revolution—with the objectionable provincial executives removed, all coercive authority in the central government abolished, and the legislatures left to their own absolute discretion. In other words, the average American farmer or trader of the day felt that the Revolution had been fought to get rid of all government but one directly under the control of the individual voters of the States. Typical of such were men like Samuel Adams of Massachusetts and Patrick Henry of Virginia. They had learned their politics in the period before the Revolution, and clung to the old colonial spirit, which regarded normal politics as essentially defensive and anti-governmental.

On the other hand, there were a good many individuals in the country who recognized that the triumph of the colonial ideal was responsible for undeniable disasters. Such men were found, especially, among the army officers and among those who had tried to aid the cause in diplomatic or civil office during the Revolution. Experience made them realize that the practical abolition of all executive authority and the absence of any real central government had been responsible for chronic inefficiency. The financial collapse, the lack of any power on the part of Congress to enforce its laws or resolutions, the visible danger that State legislatures might consult their own convenience in supporting the common enterprises or obligations—all these shortcomings led men like Washington, Hamilton, Madison, Webster, a pamphleteer of New England, to urge even before 1781 that a genuine *government* should be set up to replace the mere league. Their supporters were, however, few, and confined mainly to those merchants or capitalists who realized the necessity of general laws and a general authority. It is scarcely conceivable that the inherited prejudices of most Americans in favour of local independence could have been overborne had not the Revolution been followed by a series of public distresses, which drove to the side of the strong-government advocates—temporarily, as it proved—a great number of American voters.

When hostilities ended, the people of the United States entered upon a period of economic confusion. In the first place, trade was disorganized, since the old West India markets were lost and the privileges formerly enjoyed under the Navigation Acts were terminated by the separation of the countries. American shippers could not at once discover in French or other ports an equivalent for the former triangular trade. In the second place, British manufacturers and exporters rushed to recover their American market, and promptly put out of competition the American industries which had begun to develop during the war. Specie, plentiful for a few months, now flowed rapidly out of the country, since American merchants were no longer able to buy British goods by drawing on West India credits. At the same time, with the arrival of peace, the State courts resumed their functions, and general liquidation began; while the State legislatures, in the effort to adjust war finances, imposed what were felt to be high taxes. The result was a general complaint of hard times, poverty, and insufficient money. Some States made efforts to retaliate against Great Britain by tariffs and navigation laws, but this only damaged their own ports by driving British Trade to their neighbours'. Congress could afford no help, since it had no power of commercial regulation.

The effect upon the working of the Confederation showed that a majority of Americans had learned nothing from all their experiences, for the State legislatures declined to furnish to the central government any more money than they felt to be convenient, regardless of the fact that without their regular support the United States was certain to become bankrupt. Robert Morris was appointed Financier in 1781, and took energetic steps to introduce order into the mass of loan certificates, foreign loans, certificates of indebtedness, and mountains of paper currency; but one unescapable fact stood in his way, that the States felt under no obligation to pay their quotas of expenses. In spite of his urgent appeals, backed by resolutions of Congress, the government revenues remained too scanty to pay even the interest on the debt. Morris resigned in disgust in 1784; and his successors, a committee of Congress, found themselves able to do nothing more than confess bankruptcy. The people of the States felt too poor to support their federal government, and, what was more, felt no responsibility for its fate.

Without revenue, it naturally followed that the Congress of the Confederation accomplished practically nothing. As will be shown later, it could secure no treaties of any importance, since its impotence to enforce them was patent. It managed to disband the remaining troops with great difficulty and only under the danger of mutiny, a danger so great that it took all of Washington's personal influence to prevent an uprising at Newburg in March, 1783. For the rest, its leaders, men often of high ability —Hamilton, Madison, King of Massachusetts, Sherman of Connecticut—found themselves helpless. Naturally they appealed to the States for additional powers and submitted no less than three amendments: first, in 1781, a proposal to permit Congress to levy and collect a five per cent. duty on imports; then, in 1783, a plan by which certain specific duties were to be collected by State officers and turned over to the government; and finally, in 1784, a request that Congress be given power to exclude vessels of nations which would not make commercial treaties. No one of these succeeded, although the first plan failed of unanimous acceptance by one State only. The legislatures recognized the need, but dreaded to give any outside power whatever authority within their respective boundaries. While those who advocated these amendments kept reiterating the positive necessity for some means to avert national disgrace and bankruptcy, their opponents, reverting to the language of 1775, declared it incompatible with " liberty " that any authority other than the State's should be exercised in a State's territory. By 1787, it was clear that any hope of specific amendments was vain. Unanimity from thirteen legislatures was not to be looked for.

On the other hand, where the States chose to act they produced important results. The cessions of western lands, which had been exacted by Maryland as her price for ratifying the Articles, were carried out by New York, Massachusetts, Connecticut, and Virginia until the title to all territory west of Pennsylvania and north of the Ohio was with the Confederation. Then, although nothing in the Articles authorized such action, Congress, in 1787, adopted an Ordinance establishing a plan for settling the new lands. After a period of provincial government, substantially identical with that of the colonies, the region was to be divided into States and admitted into the union, under the terms of an annexed "compact" which prohibited slavery and guaranteed civil rights. But where the States did not co-operate, confusion reigned. Legislatures imposed such tariffs as they saw fit, which led to actual inter-State commercial discriminations between New York and its neighbours. Connecticut and Pennsylvania wrangled over land claims. The inhabitants of the territory west of New Hampshire set up a State government under the name of Vermont, and successfully maintained themselves against the State of New York,

ENGLAND AND AMERICA 137

which had a legal title to the soil, while the frontier settlers in North Carolina were prevented only by inferior numbers from carrying through a similar secession.

Finally, in the years 1785–7, the number of those who found the unrestrained self-government of the separate States another name for anarchy was enormously increased by a sudden craze for paper money, " tender " laws, and " stay " laws which swept the country. The poorer classes, especially the farmers, denounced the courts as agents of the rich, clamoured for more money to permit the easy payment of obligations, and succeeded in compelling more than half of the States to pass laws hindering the collection of debts and emitting bills of credit, which promptly depreciated. Worse remained. In New Hampshire, armed bands tried to intimidate the legislature; and in Massachusetts the rejection of such laws brought on actual insurrection. Farmers assembled under arms, courts were broken up, and a sharp little civil war, known as Shays' Rebellion, was necessary before the State government could re-establish order.

In these circumstances, a sudden strong reaction against mob rule and untrammelled democracy ran through the country, swinging all men of property and law-abiding habits powerfully in favour of the demand for a new, genuinely authoritative, national government, able to compel peace and good order. So the leaders of the reform party struck; and at a meeting of Annapolis in October, 1786, summoned originally to discuss the problem of navigating the Potomac River, they issued a call for a convention of delegates from all the States to meet at Philadelphia in May, 1787, for the purpose of recommending provisions "intended to render the federal government adequate to the exigencies of the Union." This movement, reversing the current of American his tory, gained impetus in the winter of 1787. Congress seconded the call; and, after Virginia had shown the way by nominating its foremost men as delegates, the other States fell into line and sent representatives—all but Rhode Island, which was the scene of an orgy of paper-money tyranny, and would take no part in any such meeting.

Of the fifty-five men present at the Philadelphia convention, not more than half-a dozen were of the old colonial type, which clung to individual State independence as the palladium of liberty. All the others felt that the time had come to lay the most thoroughgoing limitations upon the States, with the express purpose of preventing any future repetition of the existing inter-State wrangles, and especially of the financial abuses of the time; and they were ready to gain this end by entrusting large powers to the central government. They divided sharply, however, on one important point, namely, whether the increased powers were to be exercised by a government similar to the existing one, or by something wholly new and far more centralized; and over this question the convention ran grave danger of breaking up.

Discussion began in June, 1787, behind closed doors, with a draft plan agreed upon by the Virginia members as the working project. This was a bold scheme, calling for the creation of a single great State, relying on the people for its authority, superior to the existing States, and able, if necessary, to coerce them; in reality, a fusion of the United States into a single commonwealth. In opposition to this, the representatives of the smaller States—Delaware, New Jersey, Maryland and Connecticut—aided by the conservative members from New York, announced that they would never consent to any plan which did not safeguard the individuality and equality of their States; and, although the Virginia plan commanded a majority of those present, its supporters were obliged to permit a compromise in order to prevent an angry dissolution of the convention. In keeping with a suggestion of the

Connecticut members, it was agreed that one House of the proposed legislature should contain an equal representation of the States, while the other should be based on population.

The adoption of this compromise put an end to the danger of disruption, for all but a few irreconcilables were now ready to co-operate; and in the course of a laborious session a final draft was hammered out, with patchings, changes, and additional compromises to safeguard the interests of the plantation States in the institution of slavery.

When the convention adjourned, it placed before the people of America a document which was a novelty in the field of government. In part, it aimed to establish a great State, on the model of the American States, which in turn derived their features from the colonial governments. It had a Congress of two Houses, an executive with independent powers, and a judiciary authorized to enforce the laws of the United States. Congress was given full and exclusive power over commerce, currency, war and peace, and a long list of enumerated activities involving inter-State questions, and was authorized to pass all laws necessary and proper to the carrying out of any of the powers named in the constitution. Further, the constitution, the federal laws, and treaties were declared to be the supreme

ENGLAND AND AMERICA 141

law of the land, anything in a State law or constitution notwithstanding. In addition, the States were expressly forbidden to enter the fields reserved to the federal government, and were prohibited from infringing the rights of property. On the other hand, the new government could not exist without the co-operation of the States in providing for the election of electors,—to choose a president—of senators, and of congressmen. It was a new creation, a federal State.

There now followed a sharp and decisive contest to gain the necessary ratification by nine commonwealths. At first, the advocates of strong government, by a rapid campaign, secured the favourable votes of half-a-dozen States in quick succession; but when it came the turn of New York, Massachusetts, and Virginia, the conservative, localistic instincts of the farmers and older people were roused to make a strenuous resistance. The " Federalists," as the advocates of the new government termed themselves, had to meet charges that the proposed scheme would crush the liberties of the State, reduce them to ciphers, and set up an imitation of the British monarchy. But, by the eager urging of the foremost lawyers and most influential men of the day, the tide was turned and ratification carried, although with the utmost difficulty, and usually with the recommendation of amendments to perfect the constitution. In June, 1788, the contest ended; and, although Rhode Island and North Carolina remained unreconciled, the other eleven States proceeded to set up the new government.

In the winter of 1789, in accordance with a vote of the Congress of the Confederation, the States chose electors and senators, and the people voted for representatives. But one possible candidate existed for the presidency, namely, the hero of the Revolutionary War; and accordingly Washington received the unanimous vote of the whole electoral college. With him, John Adams was chosen vice-president, by a much smaller majority. The Congress, which slowly assembled, was finally able to count and declare the votes, the two officers were inaugurated, and the new government was ready to assume its functions.

There followed a period of rapid and fundamental legislation. In the new Congress were a body of able men, by far the greater number of them zealous to establish a strong authoritative government, and to complete the victory of the Federalists. The defeated States' Rights men now stood aside, watching their conquerors carry their plan to its conclusion. Led for the most part by James Madison of the House, Congress passed Acts creating executive departments with federal officials; establishing a full independent federal judiciary, resident in every State, with a supreme court above all; imposing a tariff for revenue and for protection to American industries, and appropriating money to settle the debts of the late confederation. In addition, it framed and submitted to the States a series of constitutional amendments whose object was to meet Anti-federalist criticisms by securing the individual against oppression from the federal government. When Congress adjourned in September, 1789, after its first session, it had completed a thoroughgoing political revolution. In place of a loose league of entirely independent States, there now existed a genuine national government, able to enforce its will upon individuals and to perform all the functions of any State.

That the American people, with their political inheritance, should have consented even by a small majority to abandon their traditional lax government, remains one of the most remarkable political decisions in history. It depended upon the concurrence of circumstances which, for the moment, forced all persons of property and law-abiding instincts to join together in all the States to remedy an intolerable situation.

The leaders, as might be expected, were a different race of statesmen, on the whole, from those who had directed events prior to 1776. Washington and Franklin favoured the change; but Richard Henry Lee and Patrick Henry were eager opponents, Samuel Adams was unfriendly, and Thomas Jefferson, in Paris, was unenthusiastic. The main work was done by Hamilton, Madison, John Marshall, Gouverneur Morris, Fisher Ames—men who were children in the days of the Stamp Act. The old agitators and revolutionists were superseded by a new type of politicians, whose interests lay in government, not opposition.

But the fundamental American instincts were not in reality changed; they had only ebbed for the moment. No sooner did Congress meet in its second session in January, 1790, and undertake the task of reorganizing the chaotic finances of the country, than political unanimity vanished, and new sectional and class antagonisms came rapidly to the front in which could be traced the return of the old-time colonial habits. The central figure was no longer Madison, but Hamilton, Secretary of the Treasury, who aspired to be a second William Pitt, and submitted an elaborate scheme for refunding the entire American debt. In addition, he called for an excise tax, and later recommended the chartering of a National Bank to serve the same function in America that the Bank of England performed in Great Britain.

Daring, far-sighted, based on the methods of English financiers, Hamilton's plans bristled with points certain to arouse antagonism. He proposed to refund and pay the debt at its face value to actual holders, regardless of the fact that the nearly worthless federal stock and certificates of indebtedness had fallen into the hands of speculators; he recommended that the United States should assume, fund, and pay the war debt of the States, disregarding the fact that, while some States were heavily burdened, others had discharged their obligations. He urged an excise tax on liquors, although such an internal tax was an innovation in America and was certain to stir intense opposition; he suggested the chartering of a powerful bank, in spite of the absence of any clause in the constitution authorizing such action. Hamilton was, in fact, a great admirer of the English constitution and political system, and he definitely intended to strengthen the new government by making it the supreme financial power and enlisting in its support all the moneyed interests of the country. Property, as in England, must be the basis of government.

Against his schemes, there immediately developed a rising opposition which made itself felt in Congress, in State legislatures, in the newspapers, and finally in Washington's own Cabinet. All the farmer and debtor elements in the country disliked and dreaded the financial manipulations of the brilliant secretary; and the Virginian planters, universally borrowers, who had been the strongest single power in establishing the new constitution, now swung into opposition to the administration. Madison led the fight in the House against Hamilton's measures; and Jefferson, in the Cabinet, laid down, in a memorandum of protest against the proposed bank, the doctrine of " strict construction " of the constitution according to which the powers granted to the federal government ought to be narrowly construed in order to preserve the State governments, the source of liberty, from encroachment. He denounced the bank, accordingly, as unwarranted by the constitution, corrupt, and dangerous to the safety of the country. In the congressional contest Hamilton was successful, for all his recommendations were adopted, but at the cost of creating a lasting antagonism in the southern States and in the western regions.

In 1791, Jefferson and Madison co-operated to establish a newspaper at Philadelphia whose sole occupation consisted in denouncing the corrupt and monarchical Secretary of the Treasury. Hamilton retorted by publishing letters charging Jefferson with responsibility for it; and Washington, who steadily approved Hamilton's policies, found his Cabinet splitting into two factions. By the year 1792, when the second presidential election took place, the opposition, styling itself " Republican," was sufficiently well organized to run George Clinton, formerly the Anti-federalist leader of New York, for the Vice-Presidency against the " monarchical" Adams. Washington was not opposed, but no other one of the Hamiltonian supporters escaped attack. There was, in short, the beginning of the definite formation of political parties on lines akin to those which existed in the period before 1787. Behind Jefferson and Madison were rallying all the colonial-minded voters, to whom government was at best an evil and to whom, under any circumstances, strong authority and elaborate finance were utterly abhorrent. Around Hamilton gathered the men whose interests lay in building up a genuine, powerful, national government — the merchants, shipowners, moneyed men and creditors generally in the northern States—and, of course, all Tories.

Up to 1793, the Federalist administration successfully maintained its ground; and, when the Virginian group tried in the House to prove laxity and mismanagement against Hamilton, he was triumphantly vindicated. Had the United States been allowed to develop in tranquillity and prosperity for a generation, it is not unlikely that the Federalist party might have struck its roots so deeply as to be impervious to attacks. But it needed time, for in contrast to the Jeffersonian party, whose origin is manifestly in the old-time colonial political habits of democracy, local independence, and love of lax finance, the Federalist party was a new creation, with no traditions to fall back upon. Reflecting in some respects British views, notably in its distrust of the masses and its respect for property and wealth, it far surpassed any English party of the period, except the small group led by William Pitt, in its demand for progressive and vigorous legislation. In 1793, when matters were in this situation, the state of European and British politics suddenly brought the United States into the current of world politics, and subjected the new administration to difficulties, which were ultimately to cause its downfall.

CHAPTER VIII

THE FIRST PERIOD OF COMMERCIAL ANTAGONISM, 1783–1795

WHILE the United States had been undergoing the important changes of the period, 1783–1793, England had passed through an almost equally significant political transformation, in course of which the two countries entered upon a long history of difficult and unfriendly diplomatic relations. The treaty of peace ended the political union of the two communities, but it left the nature of their commercial relations to be settled; and this, for the United States, was a problem second only in importance to that of federal government. If the prosperity of the thirteen States was to be restored, the old-time trade routes of the colonial days must be reestablished. The West India market for fish, grain, and lumber, the British or European market for plantation products must be replaced on a profitable basis, and the United States must be prepared to purchase these privileges by whatever concessions lay in its power to grant. It rested chiefly with England to decide whether to permit the former colonies to resume their earlier commercial system or begin a new policy, for it was with Britain and the British colonies that seven-eighths of American commerce naturally was carried on.

Unfortunately for the people of the United States, and unfortunately for the harmony of the two countries, the prevailing beliefs of English merchants, shipowners, naval authorities, and, in general, the official classes were such as to render a complete resumption of the former trade relations almost impossible. According to the political and economic doctrines underlying the Acts of Trade, the moment that the two countries became separated their interests automatically became antagonistic. American shipping, formerly fostered when under the flag, now assumed the aspect of a formidable rival to the British merchant marine and, as such, ought to be prevented from taking any profit which by any device could be turned toward British ships.

The treaty of peace had scarcely been signed when there appeared a pamphlet by Lord Sheffield, early in 1783, which won instant success, passing through several editions. This announced that henceforward it was the duty of the British government to discourage and crush American navigation to the extent of its power in order to check a dangerous rival, taking especial care to reserve the West Indies for exclusive British control. At the possibility of losing the profitable American market through retaliatory measures, Sheffield laughed in scorn. " We might as reasonably dread the effect of combinations among the German as among the American States," he sneered, " and deprecate the resolves of the Diet as those of Congress." There were elements, of course, to whom these arguments of Sheffield were unwelcome, particularly the West India planters themselves, and to a degree the British manufacturers, who would gladly have resumed the trade of the years before 1776; but, so far as the great majority of Englishmen was concerned, it seems impossible to doubt that Lord Sheffield was a true spokesman of their convictions.

In addition to the economic theories of the time, the temper of the British people was sullen, hostile, and contemptuous toward the former colonies. The bulk of the nation had come to condemn the policy of the North Ministry which had led to the loss of the plantations, but they did not love the Americans any the more for that. The sharp social distinctions, which prior to 1776 had rendered the nobility, the gentry, the clergy, and the professions contemptuous toward the colonists, still reigned unchecked; and the Tories and most of the ruling classes, regarding the Americans as a set of ungrateful and spiteful people, whom it was well to have lost as subjects, ceased to take any interest in their existence. The United States was dropped, as an unpleasant subject is banished from conversation; and the relations of the two countries became a matter of national concern only when the interests of shipowners, merchants, or naval authorities were sufficiently strong to compel attention from the governing classes.

The Whig leaders should, of course, be excepted from this general statement, for they and their followers—both their parliamentary coterie and their middle-class adherents outside—retained a friendly attitude, and tried to treat the United States with a consideration which usually had no place in Tory manners. But Whigs as well as Tories held the prevailing conceptions of naval and economic necessities, and only scattered individuals, like William Pitt, were affected by the new doctrines of Adam Smith. Their commercial policy tended to differ only in degree from that of the more rigid Tories.

To make it certain that the United States should fail to secure favourable commercial rights, the ascendancy of the Whigs came to a sudden end within a year from its beginning. The Shelburne Ministry, which made the peace, had to meet the opposition not only of the Tories but of the group led by Fox. In the session of 1783, the Whig party was thus openly split, and presently all England was scandalized to see Fox enter into a coalition with no less a person than Lord North for the purpose of obtaining office. Shelburne resigned on February 24, after the passage of a resolution of censure on the Peace; and George III, after trying every expedient to avoid what he considered a personal disgrace, was forced, on April 2, to admit Fox and North as Ministers under the nominal headship of the Duke of Portland. So Tories were restored to a share in the government, since nearly half of the coalition majority depended upon Tory votes. In December, 1783, the King, by a direct exercise of his influence, caused the Lords to throw out a Ministerial bill for the government of India and, dismissing the coalition Ministers, he appealed to William Pitt. That youthful politician, who had first entered office as Chancellor of the Exchequer under Shelburne, succeeded, after a sharp parliamentary contest, in breaking down the opposition majority in the House, and in a general election in March, 1784, won a great victory. Then, at the head of a mixed Cabinet, supported by Tories and King's Friends as well as by his own followers from among the Whigs, Pitt maintained himself, secure in the support of George III, but in no sense his agent or tool. In the next few years, he made his hold secure by his skill in parliamentary leadership and his success in carrying financial and administrative reforms. This was the first peace Ministry since that of Pelham, 1746–1754, which won prestige through efficient government. It was, however, mainly Tory in temper, and as such distinctly cold and unfriendly toward America. Pitt himself was undoubtedly in favour of liberal commercial relations; but in that respect, as in the question of parliamentary reform, he followed the opinions of his supporters and of the nation.

The British policy toward the United States, under the circumstances, was dictated by a strict adherence to the principles set forth by Lord Sheffield. Pitt, while Chancellor of the Exchequer under Shelburne, introduced a very liberal Bill, which, if enacted, would have secured full commercial reciprocity, including the West India trade. This failed to pass, however, and was abandoned when Pitt left office in April, 1783. The Fox-North Ministry followed a different plan by causing Parliament to pass a Bill authorizing the Crown to regulate the trade with the West Indies. They then, by proclamation, allowed the islands to import certain articles from the United States, not including fish or lumber, and only in British bottoms. It was hoped that Canada would take the place of the United States in supplying the West India colonies, and that British vessels would monopolize the carrying. In 1787 this action was ratified by Parliament, and the process of discouraging American shipping was adopted as a national policy. American vessels henceforward came under the terms of the Navigation Acts, and could take part only in the direct trade between their own country and England. When John Adams, in 1785, arrived at London as Minister, and tried to open the subject of a commercial treaty, he was unable to secure the slightest attention to the American requests and felt himself to be in an atmosphere of hostility and social contempt. The British policy proved in a few years fairly successful. It reduced American shipping trading with England, it drove American vessels from the British West Indies, and, owing to the impossibility of the States retaliating separately, it did not diminish the British market in America. Up to 1789, when the first Congress of the United States passed a navigation act and adopted discriminating duties, America remained commercially helpless. The profit went to British shipowners and merchants.

The American government naturally

turned to the other powers having American possessions, France and Spain, hoping to secure from them compensating advantages. So far as France was concerned, the government of Louis XVI was friendly; but its finances were in such confusion and its administration so unsteady after 1783 that Jefferson, Minister to France, could secure no important concessions save one. In 1784, as though to step into the place left vacant by the English, the French crown, by royal order, permitted direct trade between the United States and the French West Indies in vessels of less than sixty tons burden. The result was striking. In a few years the American molasses trade, driven from the British islands, took refuge at San Domingo, building up a tremendous sugar export and more than filling the place of the British trade. In 1790 the commerce of San Domingo surpassed that of all the British Islands together. Here again, French friendship shone in contrast to English antagonism. Every American shipowner felt the difference, and remembered it.

With Spain the United States was less successful. Jay, Secretary for Foreign Affairs, undertook negotiations through Diego Gardoqui, a Spaniard who, during the Revolution, had furnished many cargoes of supplies. He found that country sharply dissatisfied over the boundary assigned to the United States. The British, in ceding Florida to Spain, had not turned over all of their province of 1763, but had handed that part of it north of thirty-two degrees to the United States, and, further, had granted the latter the free navigation of the Mississippi, through Spanish territory. Gardoqui offered in substance to make a commercial treaty provided the United States would surrender the claim to navigate the Mississippi for twenty years. Jay, to whose mind the interests of the seaboard shipowners and producers far outweighed the desires of the few settlers of the interior waters, was willing to make the agreement. But an angry protest went up from the southern States, whose land claims stretched to the Mississippi, and he could secure, in 1787, a vote of only seven States to five in Congress. Since all treaties required the consent of nine States, this vote killed the negotiations. Spain remained unfriendly, and continued to intrigue with the Indian tribes in the south-western United States with a view to retaining their support.

Further north, the United States found itself mortified and helpless before British antagonism. After 1783 the country had Canada on its northern border as a small but actively hostile neighbour, for there thousands of proscribed and ruined Tories had taken refuge. The governors of Canada, Carlton and Simcoe, as well as the men commanding the frontier posts, had served against the Americans and regarded them as rivals. To secure the western fur trade and to retain a hold over the western Indians was recognized as the correct and necessary policy for Canada; and the British government, in response to Canadian suggestions, decided to retain their military posts along the Great Lakes within the boundaries of the United States. To justify them in so doing, they pointed with unanswerable truth to the fact that the United States had not carried out the provisions of the Treaty of 1783 regarding British debts, and that Tories, contrary to the letter and spirit of that treaty, were still proscribed by law. The State courts felt in no way bound to enforce the treaty, nor did State legislatures choose to carry it out. British debts remained uncollectible, and the British therefore retained their western posts and through them plied a lucrative trade with the Indians to the south of the Great Lakes.

In the years after the war, a steady flow of settlers entered the Ohio valley, resuming the movement begun before the Revolution, and took up land in Kentucky and the Northwest territory. By 1792 Kentucky

ENGLAND AND AMERICA 159

was ready to be admitted as a State, and Tennessee and Ohio were organized as territories. These settlers naturally found the Indians opposing their advance, and the years 1783–1794 are a chronicle of smouldering border warfare, broken by intermittent truces. During all this time it was the firm belief of the frontiersmen that the Indian hostility was stimulated by the British posts, and hatred of England and the English grew into an article of faith on their part. Ultimately, the new government under Washington undertook a decisive campaign. At first, in 1791, General St. Clair, invading Ohio with raw troops, was fearfully defeated, with butchery and mutilation of more than two-thirds of his force; but in 1794 General Wayne, with a more carefully drilled body, compelled the Indians to retreat. Yet with the British posts still there, a full control was impossible.

The new constitution, which gave the United States ample powers of enforcing treaties and making commercial discriminations, did not at once produce any alteration in the existing unsatisfactory situation. Spain remained steadily indifferent and unfriendly. France, undergoing the earlier stages of her own revolution, was incapable of carrying out any consistent action. The Pitt Ministry, absorbed in the game of European politics and in internal legislation, sent a Minister, Hammond, but was content to let its commercial and frontier policies continue. But when, in 1792, the French Revolution took a graver character, with the overthrow of the monarchy, and when in 1793 England joined the European powers in the war against France, while all Europe watched with horror and panic the progress of the Reign of Terror in the French Republic, the situation of the United States was suddenly changed.

In the spring of 1793 there came the news of the war between England and France, and, following it by a few days only, an emissary from the French Republic, One and Indivisible, " Citizen Edmond Genet," arrived at Charleston, South Carolina, April 15. There now exploded a sudden overwhelming outburst of sympathy and enthusiasm for the French nation and the French cause. All the remembered help of the days of Yorktown, all the tradition of British oppression and ravages, all the recent irritation at the British trade discrimination and Indian policy-coupled with appreciation of French concessions, swept crowds in every State and every town into a tempest of welcome to Genet. Shipowners rushed to apply for privateers' commissions, crowds adopted French democratic jargon and manners. Democratic clubs were formed on the model of the Jacobin society, and " Civic Feasts," at which Genet was present, made the country resound. It looked as though the United States were certain to enter the European war as an ally of France out of sheer gratitude, democratic sympathy, and hatred for England. The French Minister, feeling the people behind him, hastened to send out privateers and acted as though the United States were already in open alliance.

It now fell to the Washington administration to decide a momentous question. Regardless of the past, regardless of the British policy since the peace, was it worth while to allow the country to become involved in war at this juncture? Decidedly not. Before Genet had presented his credentials, Washington and Jefferson had framed and issued a declaration of neutrality forbidding American citizens to violate the law of nations by giving aid to either side. It was not merely caution which led to this step. The Federalist leaders and most of their followers—men of property, standing, and law-abiding habits — were distinctly shocked at the horrors of the Reign of Terror, and felt with Burke, their old friend and defender in Revolutionary days, that such liberty as the French demanded was something altogether alien to that known in the United States or in England. And as the news became more and more ghastly, the Federalists grew rapidly to regard England, with all its unfriendliness, with all its commercial selfishness, as the saving power of civilization, and France as the chief enemy on earth of God and man. The result was to precipitate the United States into a new contest, a struggle on the part of the Federalist administration, led by Hamilton and Washington, to hold back the country from being hurled into alliance with France or into war with England. In this, they had to meet the attack of the already organizing Republican party, and of many new adherents who flocked to it during the years of excitement.

The first contest was a short one. Genet, his head turned by his reception, resented the strict neutrality enforced by the administration, tried to compel it to recede, endeavoured to secure the exit of privateersmen in spite of their prohibition, and ultimately in fury appealed to the people against their government. This conduct lost him the support of even the most sanguine democrats, and, when the administration asked for his recall, he fell from his prominence unregretted. But his successor, Fauchet, a less extreme man, was warmly welcomed by the opposition leaders, including Madison and Randolph, Jefferson's successor as Secretary of State, and was admitted into the inmost councils of the party.

Hardly was Genet disposed of when a more dangerous crisis arose, caused by the naval policy of England. When war broke out, the British cruisers, as was their custom, fell upon French commerce, and especially upon such neutral commerce as could, under the then announced principles of international law, be held liable to capture. Consequently, American vessels, plying their lucrative trade with the French West Indies, were seized and condemned by British West India prize courts. It was a British dogma, known as the Rule of 1756, that if trade by a neutral with enemies' colonies had been prohibited in peace, it became contraband in time of war, otherwise belligerents, by simply opening their ports, could employ neutrals to do their trading for them. In this case, the trade between the French West Indies and America had not been prohibited in peace, but the seizures were made none the less, causing a roar of indignation from the entire American seacoast. Late in 1793, the British Ministry added fresh fuel to the fire by declaring provisions taken to French territory to be contraband of war. If an intention to force the United States into alliance with France had been guiding the

Pitt Ministry, no better steps could have been devised to accomplish the end. As a matter of fact, the Pitt Ministry thought very little about it in the press of the tremendous European cataclysm.

When Congress met in December, 1793, the old questions of Hamilton's measures and the " monarchism " of the administration were forgotten in the new crisis. Apparently a large majority in the House, led by Madison, were ready to sequester British debts, declare an embargo, build a navy, and in general prepare for a bitter contest; but by great exertions the administration managed to stave off these drastic steps by promising to send a special diplomatic mission to prevent war. During the summer the excitement grew, for it was in this year that Wayne's campaign against the western Indians took place, which was generally believed to be rendered necessary by the British retention of the posts; and also in this same summer the inhabitants of western Pennsylvania broke into insurrection against the hated excise tax. This lawlessness was attributed by the Federalists, including Washington himself, to the demoralizing influence of the French Revolution, and was therefore suppressed by no less than 15,000 militia, an action denounced by the Republicans—as Randolph confided to the French Minister—as an example of

ENGLAND AND AMERICA 165

despotic brutality. Men were fast coming to be incapable of cool thought on party questions.

The special mission to England was undertaken by the Chief Justice, Jay, the most experienced diplomat in America since the death of Franklin. Upon arriving in England, he found the country wild with excitement and horror over the French Revolution, and with all its interest concentrated upon the effort to carry on war by land and sea. The Pitt Ministry was now supported by all Tories, representing the landholding classes, the clergy, and the professions, and by nearly all the aristocratic Whigs. Burke, one-time defender of the American Revolution, was exhausting his energies in eloquent and extravagant denunciations of the French. Only a handful of radicals, led by Fox, Sheridan, and Camden, and representing a few constituents, still dared to proclaim liberal principles. In all other classes of society, democracy was regarded as synonymous with bestial anarchy and infidelity. Clearly the United States, from its very nature as a republic, could hope for no favour, in spite of the noticeably English prepossessions of Hamilton's party.

Jay dealt directly and informally with William Grenville, the Secretary for Foreign Affairs, and seems rapidly to have come to the conclusion that it was for the interest of the United States to get whatever it could, rather than to endeavour to haggle over details with an immovable and indifferent Ministry, thereby hazarding all success. On his part, Grenville clearly did his best to establish a practicable working arrangement, agreeing with Jay in so framing the treaty as to waive "principles" and "claims" and to include precise provisions. The upshot was that when Jay finished his negotiations he had secured a treaty which for the first time established a definite basis for commercial dealings and removed most of the dangerous outstanding difficulties. British debts were to be adjusted by a mixed commission, and American claims for unjust seizures in the West Indies were to be dealt with in similar fashion. The British were to evacuate the north-western military posts, and, while they did not withdraw or modify the so-called "rule of 1756," they agreed to a clear definition of contraband of war. They were also ready to admit American vessels of less than seventy tons to the British West Indies, provided the United States agreed not to export West India products for ten years. Here Jay, as in his dealings with Gardoqui, showed a willingness to make a considerable sacrifice in order to gain a definite small point. On the whole, the treaty comprised all that the Pitt Ministry, engaged in a desperate war with the French Republic, was likely to concede.

The treaty left England in the winter of 1795 and reached America after the adjournment of Congress. Although it fell far short of what was hoped for, it still seemed to Washington wholly advisable to accept it under the circumstances as an alternative to further wrangling and probable war. Sent under seal of secrecy to the Senate, in special session, its contents were none the less revealed by an opposition senator, and a tempest of disappointment and anger swept the country. In every seaport Jay was execrated as a fool and traitor and burned in effigy. Washington watched unmoved. The Senate voted ratification by a bare two-thirds, but struck out the West India article, preferring to retain the power of re-exporting French West India produce rather than to acquire the direct trade with the English islands. Washington added his signature, the British government accepted the amendment, and the treaty came into effect. The West India privilege was, in fact, granted by the Pitt Ministry, as in the treaty, owing to the demands of the West India planters. In America the storm blew itself out in a few weeks of noise and anger, and the country settled down to make the best of the privileges gained, which, however incomplete, were well worth the effort.

So the Federalist administration kept the United States neutral, and gave it at last a definite commercial status with England. It did more, for in August, 1795, the northwestern Indians, beaten in battle and deprived of the presence of their protectors, made a treaty abandoning all claims to the region south of Lake Erie. The Spanish government, on hearing of the Jay treaty, came to terms in October, 1795, agreeing to the boundaries of 1783, granting a "right of deposit" to American trades down the Mississippi at or near New Orleans, and promising to abandon Indian intrigues. The diplomatic campaign of the Federalists seemed to be crowned with general success.

But in the process the passions of the American people had become deeply stirred, and by the end of 1795 the Federalist party could no longer, as at the outset, count on the support of all the mercantile elements and all the townspeople, for, by their policy toward France and England, Washington, Hamilton, and their associates had set themselves against the underlying prejudices and beliefs of the voters. The years of the strong government reaction were at an end. The time had come to fight for party existence.

CHAPTER IX

THE TRIUMPH OF DEMOCRACY IN THE UNITED STATES, 1795–1805

With the temporary shelving of British antagonism, the Federalist administration passed its second great crisis; but it was immediately called upon to face new and equally serious differences with France which were ultimately to prove the cause of its downfall. The fundamental difficulty in the political situation in America was that the two parties were now so bitterly opposed as to render every governmental act a test of party strength. The Republicans, who accepted the leadership of Jefferson or of Clinton of New York, comprised all who favoured democracy in any sense—whether that of human equality, or local self-government, or freedom from taxes, or sympathy with France—and all who had any grievance against the administration, from frontiersmen whose cabins had not been protected against Indians or who had been forced to pay a whisky tax, to seamen whose ships had not been protected by the Jay treaty. In short, all in whom still persisted the deep-rooted colonial traditions of opposition to strong government and dislike of any but local authorities were summoned to oppose an administration on the familiar ground that it was working against their liberties by corruption, usurpation, financial burdens, and gross partisanship for England and against France.

On the other side, the Federalists were rapidly acquiring a state of mind substantially Tory in character. They were coming to dread and detest "democracy" as dangerous to the family and to society as well as to government, and to identify it with the guillotine and the blasphemies of the Worship of Reason. In the furious attacks which, after the fashion of the day, the opposition papers hurled against every act of the Federalist leaders, and which aimed as much to defile their characters as to discredit their policies, they saw a pit of anarchy yawning. Between parties so constituted, no alternative remained but a fight to a finish; and, from the moment the Federalists became genuinely anti-democratic, they were doomed. Only accident or conspicuous success on the part of their leaders could delay their destruction. A single false step on their part meant ruin.

With the ratification of the Jay treaty, a long period of peaceful relations began between England and the United States. The American shipowners quickly adapted themselves to the situation, and were soon prosperously occupied in neutral commerce. In England, American affairs dropped wholly out of public notice during the exciting and anxious years of the war of the second coalition. The Pitt Ministry ended, leaving the country under the grip of a rigid repression of all liberal thought or utterance, and was followed by the commonplace Toryism of Addington and his colleagues. Then came the Treaty of Amiens with France, the year of peace, the renewed war in 1803, and, after an interval of confused parliamentary wranglings, the return to power of Pitt in 1804, called by the voice of the nation to meet the crisis of the threatened French invasion. The United States was forgotten, diplomatic relations sank to mere routine. Such were the unquestionable benefits of the execrated treaty made by Jay and Grenville.

With France, however, American relations became suddenly strained, as a result of the same treaty. The French Republic, in the year 1795, was finally reorganized under a definite constitution as a Directorate —a republic with a plural executive of five. This government, ceasing to be merely a revolutionary body, undertook to play the game of grand politics and compelled all the neighbouring smaller States to submit to democratic revolutions, accept a constitution on the French model, and become dependent allies of the French Republic. The local democratic faction, large or small, was in each case utilized to carry through this programme, which was always accompanied with corruption and plunder to swell the revenues of France and fill the pockets of the directors and their agents. Such a policy the Directorate now endeavoured, as a matter of course, to carry out with the United States, expecting to ally themselves with the Jeffersonian party and to bribe or bully the American Republic into a lucrative alliance. The way was prepared by the infatuation with which Randolph, Jefferson, Madison, and other Republican leaders had unbosomed themselves to Fauchet, and also by an unfortunate blunder which had led Washington to send James Monroe as Minister to France in 1794. This man was known to be an active sympathizer with France, and it was hoped that his influence would assist in keeping friendly relations; but his conduct was calculated to do nothing but harm. When the news of the Jay treaty came to France, the Directorate chose to regard it as an unfriendly act, and Monroe, sharing their feelings, exerted himself rather to mollify their resentment than to justify his country.

In 1796 a new Minister, Adet, was sent to the United States to remain only in case the government should adopt a just policy toward France. This precipitated a party contest squarely on the issue of French relations. In the first place Congress, after a bitter struggle and by a bare majority, voted to appropriate the money to carry the Jay treaty into effect. This was a defeat for the French party. In the second place, in spite of a manifesto issued by Adet, threatening French displeasure, the presidential electors gave a majority of three votes for Adams over Jefferson to succeed Washington. The election had been a sharp party struggle, the whole theory of a deliberate choice by electors vanishing in the stress of partisan excitement. After this second defeat, the French Minister withdrew, severing diplomatic relations; and French vessels began to capture American merchantmen, to impress the country with the serious results of French irritation. The Washington administration now recalled Monroe and sent C. C. Pinckney to replace him, but the Directory, while showering compliments upon Monroe, refused to receive Pinckney at all and virtually expelled him from the country. In the midst of these annoying events, Washington's term closed, and the sorely tried man, disgusted with party abuse and what he felt to be national ingratitude, retired to his Virginia estates, no longer the president of the whole country, but the leader of a faction. His Farewell Address showed, under its stately phrases, his detestation of party controversy and his fears for the future.

Washington's successor, Adams, was a man of less calmness and steadiness of soul; independent, but with a somewhat petulant habit of mind, and nervously afraid of ceasing to be independent; a man of sound sense, yet of a too great personal vanity. His treatment of the French situation showed national pride and dignity as well as an adherence to the traditional Federalist policy of avoiding war. Unfortunately, his handling of the party leaders was so deficient in tact as to assist in bringing quick and final defeat upon himself and upon them.

The relations with France rapidly developed into an international scandal. Adams, supported by his party, determined to send a mission of three, including Pinckney, in order to restore friendly relations, as well as to protest against depredations and seizures which the few French cruisers at sea were now beginning to make. In the spring of 1798, however, the commission reported that its efforts had failed, and Adams was obliged to lay its correspondence before Congress. This showed that the great obstacle in the way of carrying on negotia-

ENGLAND AND AMERICA 175

tions with the French had been the persistent demands on the part of Talleyrand—the French Minister of Foreign Affairs—for a preliminary money payment, either under the form of a so-called "loan" or as a bribe outright. Such a revelation of venality struck dumb the Republican leaders who had kept asserting their distrust of Adams's sincerity and accusing the administration of injustice toward France. It took all heart out of the opposition members of Congress, and encouraged the Federalists to commit the government to actual hostilities with the hated Democrats and Jacobins. Declaring the treaties of 1778 to be abrogated, Congress authorized naval reprisals, voted money and a loan, and so began what was called a "quasi-war," since neither side made a formal declaration. Adams, riding on the crest of a brief wave of popularity, declared in a message to Congress that he would never send another Minister to France without receiving assurances that he would be received as "befitted the representative of a great, free, powerful, and independent nation." "Millions for defence, but not a cent for tribute!" became the Federalist watchword; and, when the little navy of a few frigates and sloops began to bring in French men-of-war and privateers as prizes, the country actually felt a thrill of pride and manhood. For the moment, the United States stood side by side with England in fighting the dangerous enemy of civilization. American Federalist and British Tory were at one; Adams and Pitt were carrying on the same war.

Unfortunately for the Federalists, they failed to appreciate the fundamental differences between the situation in England and in the United States, for they went on to imitate the mother country not merely in fighting the French, but in seeking to suppress what they felt to be dangerous " Jacobinical " features of American politics. In the summer of 1798, three laws were enacted which have become synonymous with party folly. Two—the Alien Acts—authorized the President at his discretion to imprison or deport any alien, friend or enemy; the third—the Sedition Act—punished by fine and imprisonment any utterance or publication tending to cause opposition to a federal law or to bring into contempt the federal government or any of its officers. Such statutes had stood in England since 1793 and were used to suppress democratic assailants of the monarchy; but such a law in the United States could mean nothing more than the suppression by Federalist courts of criticisms upon the administration made by Republican newspapers.

It furnished every opposition agitator with a deadly weapon for use against the administration; and when the Sedition Law was actually enforced, and a half-dozen Republican editors were subjected to fine or imprisonment for scurrilous but scarcely dangerous utterances, the demonstration of the inherently tyrannical nature of the Federalists seemed to be complete. It was an unpardonable political blunder.

Equally damaging to the prosperity of the Federalist party was the fact that the French Republic, instead of accepting the issue, showed a complete unwillingness to fight, and protested in public that it was having a war forced upon it. Talleyrand showered upon the United States, through every channel, official or unofficial, assurances of kindly feelings, and, so soon as he learned of Adams's demand for a suitable reception for an American Minister, gave the required assurance in his exact words. Under the circumstances, the war preparations of the Federalists became visibly superfluous, especially a provisional army which Congress had authorized under Hamilton as active commander. The opposition press and speakers denounced this as a Federalist army destined to act against the liberties of the people; and the administration could point to no real danger to justify its existence.

So high ran party spirit that the Virginian leaders thought or affected to think it necessary to prepare for armed resistance to Federalist oppression; and Madison and Jefferson, acting through the State legislatures of Virginia and Kentucky respectively, caused the adoption of two striking series of resolutions stating the crisis in Republican phraseology. In each case, after denouncing the Alien and Sedition laws as unconstitutional, the legislatures declared that the constitution was nothing more than a compact between sovereign States; that the Federal government, the creature of the compact, was not the final judge of its powers, and that in case of a palpable usurpation of powers by the Federal government it was the duty of the States to "interpose," in the words of Madison, or to "nullify" the Federal law, as Jefferson phrased it. Such language seemed to Washington, Adams, and their party to signify that the time was coming when they must fight for national existence; but to the opposition it seemed no more than a restatement of time-hallowed American principles of government, necessary to save liberty from a reactionary faction. Party hatred now rivalled that between revolutionary Whigs and Tories.

Under these circumstances the election of 1800 took place. The Federalist party

ENGLAND AND AMERICA 179

leaders, feeling the ground quaking under them, clung the more desperately to the continuance of the French "quasi-war" as their sole means for rallying popular support. But at this stage President Adams, seeing the folly of perpetuating a sham war for mere party advantage, determined to reopen negotiations. This precipitated a bitter quarrel, for the members of his Cabinet and the leading congressmen still regarded Hamilton, now a private citizen in New York, as the real leader, and followed him in urging the continuance of hostilities. Adams, unable to manage his party opponents openly, took refuge in sudden, secret, and, as they felt, treacherous conduct and sent nominations for a new French mission without consulting his advisers. The Federalist Senate, raging at Adams's stupidity, could not refuse to ratify the appointments, and so in 1799 the new mission sailed, was respectfully received by Bonaparte, and was promptly admitted to negotiations.

The Federalist party now ran straight toward defeat; for, while the leaders could not avoid supporting Adams for a second term, they hated him as a blunderer and marplot. On his part, his patience exhausted, Adams dismissed two of his secretaries, in a passion, in 1800. Later, through the wiles of Aaron Burr, Republican leader in New

York, a pamphlet, written by Hamilton to prove Adams's utter unfitness for the Presidency, was brought to light and circulated. Against this discredited and disorganized party, the Republicans, supporting Jefferson again for the Presidency and thundering against the Sedition Law, triumphantly carried a clear majority of electoral votes in the autumn; but by a sheer oversight they gave an equal number for Jefferson and for Burr, who was only intended for Vice-president. Hence under the terms of the constitution it became necessary for the House of Representatives to make the final selection, voting by States. It fell thus to the lot of the Federalist House of 1800–1801 to choose the next President, and for a while the members showed an inclination to support Burr, as at least a Northerner, rather than Jefferson. But better judgments ruled, and finally Jefferson was awarded the place which he had in fairness won. The last weeks of Federalist rule was filled with a discreditable effort to save what was possible from the wreck. New offices were established, including a whole system of circuit judgeships; and Adams spent his time up to the last hour of his term in signing commissions, stealing away in the early morning in order not to see the inauguration of his rival.

So fell the Federalist party from power. It had a brilliant record in legislation and administration; it had created a new United States; it had shown a statesmanship never equalled before or since on the American continent; but it ruined itself by endeavouring openly to establish a system of government founded on distrust of the people, and modelled after British precedents. For a few years, England and the United States approached nearer in government and policy than at any other time. But, while in England a large part of society—the nobility, gentry, middle classes, the professions, the church, and all strong political elements—supported Pitt in suppressing free speech and individual liberty, the Federalists represented only a minority, and their social principles were abhorrent to the vast majority of the inhabitants of the United States.

The Republican party, which conquered by what Jefferson considered to be a revolution no less important than that of 1776, represented a reaction to the old ideals of government traditional in colonial times, —namely as little taxation as possible, as much local independence as could exist, and the minimum of Federal authority. Jefferson professed to believe that the conduct of foreign relations was the only important function of the central government, all else properly belonging to the States. So complete was the Republican victory that the party had full power to put its principles into effect. It controlled both Houses of Congress, and was blessed with four years of peace and prosperity. Thomas Jefferson, for all his radicalism in language, was a shrewd party leader, whose actions were uniformly cautious and whose entire habit of mind favoured avoidance of any violent change. " Scientific " with the general interests of a French eighteenth - century " philosopher," he was limited in his views of public policy by his education as a Virginia planter, wholly out of sympathy with finance, commerce, or business. Under his guidance, accordingly, the United States government was subjected to what he called " a chaste reformation," rather than to a general overturning.

All expenses were cut down, chiefly at the cost of the army and navy; all appropriations were rigorously diminished, and all internal taxes were swept away. Since commerce continued active, there still remained a surplus revenue, and this Gallatin, the Secretary of the Treasury, applied to extinguishing the debt. A few of the more important Federal offices were taken from embittered Federalists and given to Republicans, but there was no general proscription of office-holders. The only action at all radical in character was the repeal of the law establishing new circuit judgeships, a step which legislated a number of Federalists out of office. The repeal was denounced by fervid Federalist orators as a violation of the constitution and a deathblow to the Union; but the appointments under the law itself had been so grossly partisan that the country was unalarmed. With these steps the Republican reaction ended. Jefferson and his party carried through no alteration of the central departments; they abandoned no Federal power except that of imposing an excise; they did not even repeal the charter of the National Bank. The real change lay in the more strictly economical finances and in the general spirit of government. The Federalist opposition, criticizing every act with bitterness and continually predicting ruin, found that under the "Jacobins" the country remained contented and prosperous and was in no more danger of atheism or the guillotine than it had been under Adams. So matters went on, year after year, the Federal government playing its part quietly and the American people carrying on their vocations in peace and prosperity.

Jefferson's general theory of foreign affairs was based on the idea that diplomacy was mainly a matter of bargain and sale, with national commerce as the deciding factor. He believed so firmly that national self-interest would lead all European powers to make suitable treaties with the United States that he considered the navy as wholly superfluous, and would have been glad to sell it. But when circumstances arose calling for a different sort of diplomacy, he was ready to modify his methods; and he so far recognized the unsuitability of peaceful measures in dealing with the Barbary corsairs as to permit the small American navy to carry on extensive operations during 1801–3, which ended in the submission of Tripoli and Algiers.

Simultaneously, Jefferson was brought face to face with a diplomatic crisis, arising from the peculiar actions of his old ally, France. At the outset of his administration, he found the treaty made by Adams's commissioners in 1800 ready for ratification, and thus began his career with all questions settled, thanks to his predecessor. But he had been in office only a few months when the behaviour of the Spanish officials at New Orleans gave cause for alarm; for they suddenly terminated the right of deposit, granted in 1795. It was quickly rumoured that the reason was to be found in the fact that France, now under the First Consul, Napo-

ENGLAND AND AMERICA 185

leon, had regained Louisiana. It was, in fact, true. Bonaparte overthrew the Directory in 1799 and established himself, under the thin disguise of "First Consul," as practical military despot in France. He had immediately embraced the idea of establishing a western colonial empire, which should be based on San Domingo, now controlled by insurgent negroes, and which should include Louisiana. By a treaty of October 1, 1800, he compelled Spain to retrocede the former French province in return for a promise to establish a kingdom of "Etruria" for a Spanish prince. During 1802 large armaments sailed to San Domingo and began the process of reconquest. It needed only the completion of that task for Napoleon to be ready to take over Louisiana, and thereby to gain absolute control over the one outlet from the interior territories of the United States.

Jefferson at once recognized the extreme gravity of the situation. During the years after the English, Spanish, and Indian treaties, emigrants had steadily worked their way into the inner river valleys. Western New York and Pennsylvania were rapidly filling, Ohio was settled up to the Indian treaty line, Kentucky and Tennessee were doubling in population, and fringes of pioneer communities stretched along the Ohio and Mississippi rivers. In 1796 Tennessee was admitted as a State, and Ohio was now, in 1801, on the point of asking admission. For France to shut the only possible outlet for these communities would be a sentence of economic death; and Jefferson was so deeply moved as to write to Livingston, his Minister to France, that if the rumour of the cession were true, " We must marry ourselves to the British fleet and nation." The United States must fight rather than submit. He sent Monroe to France, instructed to buy an outlet, but the latter only arrived in time to join with Livingston in signing a treaty for the purchase of the whole of Louisiana.

This startling event was the result of the failure of Napoleon's forces to reconquer San Domingo. Foreseeing the loss of Louisiana in case of the probable renewal of war with England, and desirous of money for immediate use, the Corsican adventurer suddenly threw Louisiana into the astonished hands of Livingston and Monroe. He had never, it is true, given Spain the promised compensation; he had never taken possession, and he had promised not to sell it; but such trifles never impeded Napoleon, nor, in this case, did they hinder Jefferson. When the treaty came to America, Congress was quickly convened, the Senate voted to ratify, the money was appropriated, and the whole vast region was bought for the sum of sixty million francs. Jefferson himself, the apostle of a strict construction of the constitution, could not discover any clause authorizing such a purchase; but his party was undisturbed, and the great annexation was carried through, Jefferson acquiescing in the inconsistency.

The chagrin of the Federalists at this enormous south-westward extension of the country was exceeded only by their alarm when an attempt was made to eject certain extremely partisan judges from their offices in Pennsylvania and on the Federal bench by the process of impeachment. In the first two cases the effort was successful, one Pennsylvania judge and one Federal district judge being ejected; but when, in 1805, the attack was aimed at the Pennsylvania supreme justices and at Justice Chase of the United States Supreme Court, the process broke down. The defence of the accused judges was legally too strong to be overcome, and each impeachment failed. With this the last echo of the party contest seemed to end, for by this time the Federalists were too discredited and too weak to make a political struggle. Their membership in Congress had shrunk to small figures, they had lost State after State, and in 1804 they practically let Jefferson's re-election go by default. He received all but fourteen electoral votes, out of 176. Some of the New England leaders plotted secession, but they were not strong enough for that. The party seemed dead. In 1804 its ablest mind, Hamilton, was killed in a duel with Burr, the Vice-president, and nobody remained capable of national leadership.

So the year 1805 opened in humdrum prosperity and national self-satisfaction. Jefferson could look upon a country in which he held a position rivalled only by that of a European monarch or an English prime minister. The principles of Republican equality, of States' rights, of economy and retrenchment, of peace and local self-government seemed triumphant beyond reach of attack. While Europe resounded with battles and marches, America lived in contented isolation, free from the cares of unhappy nations living under the ancient ideals.

CHAPTER X

THE SECOND PERIOD OF COMMERCIAL ANTAGONISM, 1805–1812

In the year 1805, the happy era of Republican prosperity and complacency came suddenly and violently to an end, for by this time forces were in operation which drew the United States, in utter disregard of Jefferson's theories, into the sweep of the tremendous political cyclone raging in Europe. In 1803, Napoleon forced England into renewed war, and for two years endeavoured by elaborate naval manœuvres to secure control of the Channel for a sufficient time to permit him to transport his "Grand Army" to the British shore. In 1805, however, these plans broke down; and the crushing defeat of the allied French and Spanish navies at Trafalgar marked the end of any attempt to challenge British maritime supremacy. The great military machine of the French army was then turned eastward against the armies of the coalition which England, under Pitt, was forming; and in a series of astonishing campaigns it was used to beat down the Austrians in 1805 at Austerlitz; to overwhelm the Prussians in 1806 at Jena and Auerstadt; and to force the Russians, after a severe winter campaign in East Prussia, to come to terms in 1807. Napoleon and the Tsar, Alexander, meeting on the bridge at Tilsit, July 7, divided Europe between them by agreeing upon a policy of spheres of interest, which left Turkey and the Orient for Russian expansion and all the beaten western monarchies for French domination. The Corsican captain, trampling on the ruins both of the French monarchy and the French Republic, stood as the most terrible and astounding figure in the world, invincible by land, the master of Europe.

But the withdrawal of the French from any attempt to contest the sea left England the equally undisputed master of all oceans, and rendered the French wholly dependent upon neutral nations for commerce. As French conquests led to annexations of territory in Italy and in Germany, these regions also found themselves unable to import with their own vessels, and so neutral commerce found ever-increasing markets dependent upon its activity. Now the most energetic maritime neutral power was the United States, whose merchantmen hastened to occupy the field left vacant by the practical extinction of the French carrying trade. Until 1807 they shared this with the Scandinavian countries; but after that year Napoleon, by threats and the terror

ENGLAND AND AMERICA 191

of his name, forced an unwelcome alliance upon all the States of Europe, and the United States became the sole important neutral.

In these circumstances, the merchant shipping of the United States flourished enormously, the more especially since, by importing and immediately re-exporting West India products from the French islands, Yankee skippers were able to avoid the dangerous "Rule of 1756," and to send sugar and cocoa from French colonies to Europe and England under the guise of American produce. By 1805, the whole supply of European sugar was carried in American bottoms, to the enormous profit of the United States. American ships also shared largely in the coasting trade of Europe, carrying goods between ports where British ships were naturally excluded. In fact, the great prosperity and high customs receipts to which the financial success of the Jeffersonians was due depended to a great extent on the fortunate neutral situation of the United States.

By 1805, the British shipowners felt that flesh and blood could not endure the situation. Here were France and her allies easily escaping the hardships of British naval pressure by employing neutrals to carry on their trade. Worse still, the Americans, by the device of entering and clearing

French sugar at an American port, were now able calmly to take it to England and undersell the West Indian planters in their own home markets. Pamphleteers began to criticize the government for permitting such unfair competition, Lord Sheffield, as in 1783, leading the way. In October, 1805, James Stephen, a far abler writer, summed up the anger of the British ship-owners and naval officers in a pamphlet entitled, "War in disguise, or the Frauds of the Neutral Trade." He asserted that the whole American neutral commerce was nothing more or less than an evasion of the Rule of 1756 for the joint benefit of France and the United States, and he called upon the government to put a stop to this practical alliance of America with Napoleon. This utterance seems to have made a profound impression; for a time Stephen's views became the fixed beliefs of influential public men as well as of the naval and shipowning interests.

The first steps indicating British restlessness were taken by the Pitt Ministry, which began, in 1804, a policy of rigid naval search for contraband cargoes, largely carried on off American ports. Whatever friendly views Pitt may once have entertained toward the Americans, his Ministry now had for its sole object the contest with

France and the protection of British interests. In July, 1805, a severe blow was suddenly struck by Sir William Scott, who as chief Admiralty judge rendered a decision to the effect that French sugar, entered at an American custom-house and re-exported with a rebate of the duty, was good prize under the Rule of 1756. This placed all American re-exportation of French West Indian produce at the mercy of British cruisers; and the summer of 1805 saw a sudden descent of naval officers upon their prey, causing an outcry of anger from every seaport between Maine and Maryland. The day of reckoning had come, and Jefferson and Madison, his Secretary of State, were compelled to meet the crisis. Fortunately, as it appeared, for the United States, the Pitt Ministry ended with the death of its leader on January 23, 1806, and was succeeded by a coalition in which Lord Grenville, author of the Jay treaty, was prime Minister, and Fox, an avowed friend of America, was Foreign Secretary. While it was not reasonably to be expected that any British Ministry would throw over the traditional naval policy of impressments or venture to run directly counter to shipping interests, it was open to anticipation that some such compromise as the Jay treaty might be agreed upon, which would relieve the United

States from arbitrary exactions during the European war. The Grenville Ministry showed its good intentions by abandoning the policy of captures authorized by Scott, and substituting, on May 16, 1806, a blockade of the French coast from Ostend to the Seine. This answered the purpose of hindering trade with France without raising troublesome questions, and actually allowed American vessels to take sugar to Northern Europe.

Between 1804 and 1806, Jefferson had brought the United States to the verge of war with Spain through insisting that Napoleon's cession of Louisiana had included West Florida. At the moment when British seizures began, he was attempting at once to frighten Spain by warlike words and, by a payment of two million dollars, to induce France to compel Spain to acknowledge the American title to the disputed territory. For a number of years, therefore, and until the scheme fell through, Jefferson cultivated especially friendly relations with the government of Napoleon, not from any of the former Republican enthusiasm, but solely on diplomatic grounds. Hence, although nominally neutral in the great war, he bore the appearance of a French partisan.

Jefferson felt that he had in his possession a thoroughly adequate means to secure favourable treatment from England, by simply threatening commercial retaliation. The American trade, he believed, was so necessary to the prosperity of England that for the sake of retaining it that country would make any reasonable concession. That there was a basis of truth in this belief it would be impossible to deny; for England consumed American cotton and exported largely to American markets. With this trade cut off, manufacturers and exporters would suffer, as they had suffered in the revolutionary period. But Jefferson ignored what every American merchant knew, that military and naval considerations weighed fully as heavily with England as mercantile needs, and that a country which had neither a ship-of-the-line, nor a single army corps in existence, commanded, in an age of world warfare, very slight respect. Jefferson's prejudice against professional armed forces and his ideal of war as a purely voluntary matter, carried on as in colonial times, was sufficiently proclaimed by him to be well understood across the Atlantic. Openly disbelieving in war, avowedly determined not to fight, he approached a nation struggling for life with the greatest military power on earth, and called upon it to come to terms for business reasons.

His first effort was made by causing Congress to pass a Non-importation Act, excluding certain British goods, which was not to go into effect until the end of 1806. With this as his sole weapon, he sent Monroe to make a new treaty, demanding free commerce and the cessation of the impressment of seamen from American vessels in return for the continued non-enforcement of the Non-importation Act. Such a task was more difficult than that laid upon Jay twelve years before; and Monroe, in spite of the fact that he was dealing with the same Minister, failed to accomplish even so much as his predecessor. From August to December he negotiated, first with Lord Holland, then, after Fox's death, with Lord Howick; but the treaty which he signed on December 1, 1806, contained not one of the points named in his instructions. Monroe found the British willing to make only an agreement like the Jay treaty which, while containing special provisions to render the situation tolerable, should refuse to yield any British contentions. That was the Whig policy as much in 1806 as it had been in 1766. The concessions were slight; and the chief one, regarding the re-exportation of French West Indian produce, permitted it only on condition that the goods were *bona fide* of American ownership, and had paid in the United States a duty of at least two per cent. Jefferson

ENGLAND AND AMERICA 197

did not even submit the treaty to the Senate.

After this failure, the situation grew graver. Napoleon, in December, 1806, issued from Berlin a decree declaring that, in retaliation for the aggressions of England upon neutral commerce, the British Isles were in blockade and all trade with them was forbidden. British goods were to be absolutely excluded from the continent. The reply of the Grenville Ministry to this was an Order in Council, January, 1807, prohibiting neutral vessels from trading between the ports of France or her allies; but this was denounced as utterly weak by Perceval and Canning in opposition. In April, 1807, the Grenville Ministry, turned out of office by the half insane George III, was replaced by a thoroughly Tory cabinet, under the Duke of Portland, whose chief members in the Commons were George Canning and Spencer Perceval, Foreign Secretary and Chancellor of the Exchequer respectively. The United States was now to undergo treatment of a new kind at the hands of Tories who despised its institutions, felt only contempt for the courage of its government, and were guided as regards American commerce by the doctrines of Lord Sheffield and James Stephen.

An Order in Council of November 11,

1807, drafted by Perceval and endorsed by all the rest of the Cabinet, declared that no commerce with France or her allies was henceforward to be permitted unless it had passed through English ports. To this Napoleon retorted by the Milan Decree of December, 1807, proclaiming that all vessels which had been searched by British, or which came by way of England, were good prize. Henceforth, then, neutral commerce was positively prohibited. The merchantmen of the United States could continue to trade at all only by definitely siding with one power or the other. The object of the British order was declared to be retaliation on Napoleon. Its actual effect was to place American trade once more under the rule of the Navigation Acts. As in the days before 1776, American vessels must make England their "staple" or "entrepôt," and could go only where permitted to by British orders under penalty of forfeiture. This measure was sharply attacked in Parliament by the Whigs, especially by Grenville and Howick, of the late Ministry, but was triumphantly sustained by the Tories.

At this time the chronic grievance of the impressment of seamen from American vessels grew suddenly acute. In the years of the great war, the American merchant marine, with its safe voyages and good pay, offered a highly attractive prospect for English sailors, who dreaded the danger, the monotony, and the severe discipline of British men-of-war. They swarmed by thousands into American service, securing as rapidly as possible, not infrequently by fraudulent means, the naturalization papers by which they hoped to escape the press-gang. Ever since 1793 British naval officers, recognizing no right of expatriation, had systematically impressed British seamen found on American ships and, owing to the difficulty in distinguishing the two peoples, numerous natives of New England and the middle States found themselves imprisoned on the " floating hell " of a British ship-of-the-line in an epoch when brutality characterized naval discipline. In August, 1807, the United States was stirred to fury over the forcible seizure by the British *Leopard* of three Englishmen from the U.S.S. *Chesapeake*, which, unprepared for defence, had to suffer unresisting. So hot was the general anger that Jefferson could easily have led Congress into hostile measures, if not an actual declaration of war, over the multiplied seizures and this last insult.

But Jefferson clung to peace, and satisfied himself by ordering British men-of-war out of American ports and sending a demand for reparation, with which he linked a renunciation of the right of impressment. When Congress met in December, he induced it to pass a general embargo, positively prohibiting the departure of American vessels to foreign ports. Since at the same time the Non-importation Act came into effect, all imports and exports were practically suspended. His idea was that the total cessation of American commerce would inflict such discomfort upon British and French consumers that each country would be forced to abandon its oppressive measures.

Rarely has a country, at the instance of one man, inflicted a severer strain upon its citizens. The ravages of French and English together, since the outbreak of war in 1793, did not do so much damage as the embargo did in one year, for it threatened ruin to every shipowner, importer, and exporter in the United States. Undoubtedly Jefferson and his party had in mind the success of the non-importation agreements against the Stamp Act and the Townshend duties, but what was then the voluntary action of a great majority was now a burden imposed by one part of the country upon another. The people of New York and New England simply would not obey the Act. To enforce it against Canada became an impossibility, and to prevent vessels from escaping a matter of great difficulty. Jefferson persisted doggedly, and induced Congress to pass laws giving revenue collectors extraordinary powers of search and seizure, but without results.

Under this intolerable grievance, the people of the oppressed regions rapidly lost their enthusiasm for the Democratic administration. Turning once more to the Federalist party, which had seemed practically extinct, they threw State after State into its hands, and actually threatened the Republican control in the Presidential election of 1808. Had a coalition been arranged between the disgusted Republican factions of New York and Pennsylvania and the Federalists of New England, Delaware, and Maryland, James Madison might well have been beaten for successor to Jefferson. But worse remained behind. The outraged New Englanders, led by Timothy Pickering and others, began to use again, in town-meetings and legislatures, the old-time language of 1774, once employed against the Five Intolerable Acts, and to threaten secession. As Jefferson said later, "I felt the foundations of the government shaken under my feet by the New England townships."

By this time, it was definitely proved that as a means of coercion the embargo was worthless. English manufacturers and their workmen complained, but English shipowners profited, and crowds of British seamen returned perforce to their home, even at times into the royal navy. Canning, for the Portland Ministry, sarcastically declined to be moved, observing that the embargo, whatever its motives, was practically the same as Napoleon's system, and England could not submit to being driven to surrender to France even to regain the American market or relieve the Americans from their self-inflicted sufferings. Napoleon now gave an interesting taste of his peculiar methods, for on April 17, 1808, he issued the Bayonne Decree, ordering the confiscation of all American vessels found in French ports, on the ground that, since the embargo prohibited the exit of American ships, these must, in reality, be English! Thus he gathered in about eight million dollars' worth. The policy had to be abandoned, and in the utmost ill-humour Congress repealed the embargo, on March 1, 1809, substituting non-intercourse with England and France. Thus Jefferson left office under the shadow of a monumental failure. His theory of commercial coercion had completely broken down; and he had damaged his own and his party's prestige to such an extent that the moribund Federalist organization had sprung to life and threatened the existence of the Union.

From this time onward, the New Englanders assumed the character of ultra-admirers of Great Britain. True, their vessels suffered from British seizures; but no British confiscations had done them such harm as the embargo, or taken such discreditable advantage of a transparent pretext as the Bayonne Decree. Belonging to the wealthy classes, they admired and respected England as defender of the world's civilization against Napoleon, and they detested Jefferson and Madison as tools of the enemy of mankind. They justified impressments, spoke respectfully of the British doctrines of trade, and corresponded freely with British public men. They stood, in short, exactly where the Republicans had stood in 1793, supporters of a foreign power with which the Federal administration was in controversy. In Congress and outside, they made steady, bitter menacing attacks on the integrity and honesty of the Republicans.

Under Jefferson's successor, the policy of commercial pressure was carried to its impotent conclusion. At first the action of the British government seemed to crown Madison with triumph. In the winter of 1809, the majority in Congress had talked freely of substituting war for the embargo; and at the same time the Whigs in Parliament, led by Grenville, had attacked Canning for his insolence toward the United States as likely to cause war. Whitbread called attention to the similarity between the conditions in 1809 and 1774, when " the same infatuation seemed to prevail," the same certainty existed that the Americans would not fight, and the same confident assertions were made that they could not do without England. The comparison possessed much truth, for the Tories of 1809 were as indifferent to American feelings as those of 1774, and pushed their commercial policy just as North had done his political system, in the same contemptuous certainty that the Americans would never fight. Yet Canning showed sufficient deference to his assailants to instruct Erskine, British Minister at Washington, to notify Madison that the Orders would be withdrawn in case the United States kept its non-intercourse with France, recognized the Rule of 1756, and authorized British men-of-war to enforce the Non-intercourse Act.

The immediate result was surprising, for Erskine, eager to restore harmony, did not disclose or carry out his instructions, but accepted the continuance by the United States of non-intercourse against France as a sufficient concession. He announced that the Orders in Council would be withdrawn on June 10; Madison in turn promptly issued a proclamation reopening trade, and swarms of American vessels rushed across the Atlantic. But Canning, in harsh language, repudiated the arrangement of his over-sanguine agent, and Madison was forced to the mortifying step of reimposing non-intercourse by a second proclamation. Still worse remained, for when F. J. Jackson, the next British Minister, arrived, the President had to undergo the insult of being told that he had connived with Erskine in violating his instructions. The refusal to hold further relations with the blunt emissary was a poor satisfaction. All this time, moreover, reparation for the *Chesapeake* affair was blocked, since it had been coupled with a demand for the renunciation of impressments, something that no British Ministry would have dared to yield.

On the part of Napoleon, the Non-intercourse Act offered another opportunity for plunder. When he first heard of Erskine's concessions, he was on the point of meeting them, but on learning of their failure he changed about, commanded the sequestration of all American vessels entering European ports, and in May, 1810, by the Rambouillet Decree, he ordered their confiscation and sale. The ground assigned was that the Non-intercourse Act forbade any French or English vessel to enter American ports under penalty of confiscation.

None had been confiscated, but they might be. Hence he acted. Incidentally he helped to fill his treasury, and seized about ten millions of American property.

By this time it was clear to most Americans that, however unfriendly the British policy, it was honesty itself compared to that of the Emperor, whose sole aim seemed to be to ensnare American vessels for the purpose of seizing them. The Federalists in Congress expatiated on his perfidy and barefaced plunder, but nothing could shake the intention of Madison to stick to commercial bargaining. Congress now passed another Act, destined to be the last effort at peaceful coercion. Trade was opened, but the President was authorized to reimpose non-intercourse with either nation if the other would withdraw its decrees. This Act, known always as the Macon Bill No. 2, became law in May, 1810, and Napoleon immediately seized the occasion for further sharp practice. He caused an unofficial, unsigned letter to be shown to the American Minister at Paris stating that the French decrees would be withdrawn on November 2, 1810, " it being understood that the English should withdraw theirs by that time or the United States should cause its rights to be respected by England." Madison accordingly reimposed non-intercourse with

England on the date named, and considered the French decrees withdrawn. The situation was regarded by him as though he had entered into a contract with Napoleon, which compelled him to assert that the decrees were at an end, although he had no other evidence than the existence of the situation arising from the Macon Bill.

There followed a period during which the American Minister at London, William Pinkney, endeavoured without success to convince the British government that the decrees actually were withdrawn. The Portland Ministry had fallen in 1809, and the sharp-tongued Canning was replaced in the Foreign Office by the courteous Marquess Wellesley; but Spencer Perceval, author of the Orders in Council, was Prime Minister and stiffly determined to adhere to his policy. James Stephen and George Rose, in Parliament, stood ready to defend them, and the Tory party as a whole accepted their necessity. When, therefore, Pinkney presented his request to Wellesley, the latter naturally demanded something official from Napoleon, which neither Pinkney nor Madison could supply. Finally, in February, 1811, Pinkney broke off diplomatic relations and returned home, having played his difficult part with dignity. To aggravate the situation Napoleon's cruisers continued, whenever they had a chance, to seize and burn American vessels bound for England, and his port authorities to sequester vessels arriving from England. The decrees were not in fact repealed.

Madison had committed himself, however, to upholding the honour of Napoleon—a task from which any other man would have recoiled—and the United States continued to insist on a fiction. Madison's conduct in this affair was that of a shrewd lawyer-like man who tried to carry on diplomacy between two nations fighting to the death as though it were a matter of contracts, words and phrases of legal meaning. To Napoleon, legality was an incomprehensible idea. To the Tory ministries, struggling to maintain their country against severe economic pressure, facts, not words, counted, and facts based on naval force. Upon the Jeffersonian and Madisonian attempts at peaceful coercion they looked with mingled annoyance and contempt, believing, as they did, that the whole American policy was that of a weak and cowardly nation trying by pettifogging means to secure favourable trade conditions. The situation had reached a point where the United States had nothing to hope from either contestant, by continuing this policy.

At this juncture a new political force

appeared. By 1811 the old-time Republican leaders, trained in the school of Jeffersonian ideals, were practically bankrupt. Faction paralyzed government, and Congress seemed, by its timid attitude, to justify the taunt of Quincy of Massachusetts that the Republican party could not be kicked into a war. But there appeared on the stage a new sort of Republican. In the western counties of the older States and in the new territories beyond the mountains, the frontier element, once of small account in the country and wholly disregarded under the Federalists, was multiplying, forming communities and governments, where the pioneer habits had created a democracy that was distinctly pugnacious. Years of danger from Indians, of rivalry with white neighbours over land titles, of struggle with the wilderness, had produced a half-lawless and wholly self-assertive type of man, as democratic as Jefferson himself, but with a perfect willingness to fight and with a great respect for fighters. To these men, the tameness with which the United States had submitted to insults and plundering was growing to be unendurable. Plain masculine anger began to obscure other considerations.

These Western men, moreover, had a special cause for indignation with England, which was ignored by the sea-coast communities, in the close connection which they firmly believed to exist between the British administration of upper Canada and the north-western Indians. In the years after 1809, the Indian question again began to assume a dangerous form. Settlers were coming close to the treaty lines, and, to satisfy their demands for the bottom lands along the Wabash River, Governor Harrison of Indiana Territory made an extensive series of land purchases from the small tribes on the coveted territory.

But there now appeared two remarkable Indians, Tecumseh and his brother, the Prophet, of the Shawnee tribe, who saw in the occupation of the red men's hunting lands and the inroads of frontier corn whiskey the death of all their race. These leaders began to hold their own tribe together against the purchase of whiskey or the sale of lands; then, with wider vision, they tried to organize an alliance of all the north-western Indians to prevent further white advance. They even went so far as to visit the south-western Indians, Creeks and Cherokees, to induce them to join in the grand league. The very statesmanship involved in this vast scheme rendered it dangerous in the eyes of all Westerners, who were firmly convinced that the backing of

ENGLAND AND AMERICA 211

this plan came from the British posts in Canada. There was, in reality, a good understanding between the Canadian officers and the Shawnee chiefs. In 1811 hostilities broke out at Tippecanoe, where Governor Harrison had a sharp battle with the Shawnees; but Tecumseh exerted himself to restore peaceful relations, although the frontier was in great excitement.

From the States of Kentucky, Ohio, and Tennessee, and from the inner counties of the southern States there came to the first session of the Eleventh Congress, in December, 1811, a group of young politicians—Henry Clay, John Calhoun, Langdon Cheves, Felix Grundy—who felt that the time for talk was at an end. Unless England immediately revoked its decrees, ceased impressing seamen, and refrained from instigating Indian plots there must be war. Assuming control of the House, with Clay in the Speaker's chair, they transformed the Republican party and the policy of the country. They pushed through measures for raising troops, arming ships, and borrowing money. Congress rang with fiery speeches, as month after month went by and the Perceval Ministry obstinately refused to stir from its commercial policy.

Yet the feeling of the English public was already undergoing a change. By 1812 the pretence that the Orders in Council were maintained for the purpose of starving out France was growing transparent when thousands of licences, granted freely to British vessels, permitted a vast fleet to carry on the supposedly forbidden trade. Although Perceval and Canning still insisted in Parliament that the Orders were retaliatory, the fact was patent that their only serious effect was to cause the loss of the American trade and the American market. At the threat of war, the exporters of England, suffering severely from glutted markets, began a vigorous agitation against Perceval's policy and bombarded the Ministry, through Henry Brougham, with petitions, memorials, and motions which put the Tories on the defensive. Speakers like Alexander Baring held up the system of Orders in Council as riddled with corruption, and only the personal authority of Perceval and Castlereagh kept the majority firm. At the height of this contest, Perceval was assassinated, on May 11, 1812; and it was not until June 8 that hope of a new coalition was abandoned, and the Tory Cabinet was definitely reorganized under Lord Liverpool. Almost the first act of that Ministry was to bow before the storm of petitions, criticisms, and complaints, and to announce on June 16 that they had decided to suspend the Orders.

ENGLAND AND AMERICA

Thus the very contingency upon which Jefferson and Madison had counted came to pass. The British government, at the instance of the importing and manufacturing classes, yielded to the pressure of American commercial restrictions. It was true that the danger of war weighed far more, apparently, than the Non-intercourse Act; but had there been an Atlantic cable, or even a steam transit, at that time, or had the Liverpool Ministry been formed a little earlier, the years 1807–1812 might have passed into history as a triumphant vindication of Jefferson's theories.

But it was too late. Madison, seeing, apparently, that his plans were a failure, fell in with the new majority, and after deliberate preparation sent a message to Congress in June, 1812, which was practically an invitation to declare war. In spite of the bitter opposition of all Federalists and many eastern Republicans, Congress, by the votes of the southern and western members, adopted a declaration of war on June 18, committing the United States to a contest with the greatest naval power in the world on the grounds of the Orders in Council, the impressment of seamen, and the intrigues with the north-western Indians. At the moment when Napoleon, invading Russia, began his last stroke for universal empire, the United

States entered the game as his virtual ally. This was something the Federalists could not forgive. They returned to their homes, execrating the war as waged in behalf of the arch-enemy of God and man, as the result of a pettifogging bit of trickery on the part of Napoleon. They denounced the ambitions of Clay and the Westerners, who predicted an easy conquest of Canada, as merely an expression of a pirate's desire to plunder England of its colonies, and they announced their purpose to do nothing to assist the unrighteous conflict. In their anger at Madison, they were even willing to vote for De Witt Clinton of New York, who ran for President in 1812 as an Independent Republican; and the coalition carried the electoral vote of every State north of Maryland except Pennsylvania and Vermont.

When the news of the repeal of the Orders in Council crossed the Atlantic, some efforts were made by the governor-general of Canada to arrange an armistice, hoping to prevent hostilities. But Madison does not seem to have seriously considered abandoning the war, even though the original cause had been removed. Feeling the irresistible pressure of the southern and western Democrats behind him, he announced that the contest must go on until England should abandon the practice of impressment. So the last hope of peace disappeared.

The war thus begun need never have taken place, had the Tory Ministries of Portland or Perceval cared to avert it. The United States only lashed itself into a warlike mood after repeated efforts to secure concessions, and after years of submission to British rough handling. During all this time, either Madison or Jefferson would gladly have accepted any sort of compromise which did not shut American vessels wholly out from some form of independent trade. But the enmity of the British shipowners and naval leaders and the traditional British commercial policy joined with contempt for the spiritless nation to prevent any such action until the fitting time had gone by.

CHAPTER XI

THE WAR FOR "SAILORS' RIGHTS" AND WESTWARD EXPANSION, 1812–1815

THE second war between the United States and the mother country, unlike the first, was scarcely more than a minor annoyance to the stronger party. In the years 1812–1814, England was engaged in maintaining an army in Spain, in preying on French commerce by blockade and cruising, and was spending immense sums to subsidize the European nations in their final struggle against Napoleon. The whole military and financial strength of the country, the whole political and diplomatic interest were absorbed in the tremendous European contest. Whig and Tory, landowner, manufacturer, and labourer were united in unbending determination to destroy the power of the Corsican. The Liverpool Ministry contained little of talent, and no genius, but the members possessed certain traits which sufficed to render others unnecessary, namely, an unshakable tenacity and steady hatred of the French. The whole country stood behind them on that score.

In these circumstances, the English, when obliged to fight the United States, were at liberty to send an overwhelming naval force to blockade or destroy American commerce, but were in great straits to provide men to defend Canada. It was not until a full year after the declaration of war that any considerable force of regular troops could be collected and sent there, and not for two years that anything approaching a genuine army could be directed against America.

The defence of Canada had to be left to the efforts of some few officers and men and such local levies as could be assembled.

On the side of the United States, the war was bound to take the form of an effort to capture all or part of Canada, for that was the only vulnerable British possession. On the sea the United States could hope at most to damage British commerce by means of the few national cruisers and such privateers as the shipowners of the country could send out. Without a single ship-of-the-line and with only five frigates, there existed no possibility of actually fighting the British navy. But on land it seemed as though a country with a population of over seven millions ought to be able to raise armies of such size as to overrun, by mere numbers, the slender resources of Canada; and it was the confident expectation of most of the western leaders that within a short time the whole region would be in American hands. "The acquisition of Canada this year," wrote Jefferson, "as far as the neighbourhood of Quebec, will be a mere matter of marching, and will give us experience for the attack on Halifax, the next and the final expulsion of England from the American continent."

Unfortunately for the success of these dreams, the policy of the Republican administrations had been such as to set up insuperable difficulties. The regular army, reduced under Jefferson's "passion for peace" to a bare minimum, was scattered in a few posts; the War Department was without means for equipping, feeding, and transporting bodies of troops; the whole mechanism of war administration had to be created. Further, the Secretary of the Army and nearly all the generals were elderly men, veterans of the Revolutionary Army, who had lost whatever energy they once possessed. The problem of war finances was rendered serious by the fact that revenue from the tariff, the sole important source of income, was sure to be cut off by the British naval power. The National Bank had been refused a new charter in 1811, and the government, democratic in its finances as in other matters, relied upon a hundred odd State banks of every degree of solvency for aid in carrying on financial operations.

The temper of the American people was exactly what it had been in colonial days. They regarded war as a matter to be carried on at the convenience of farmers and others, who were willing to serve in defence of their homes, but strongly objected to enlisting for any length of time. On the more pugnacious frontier, the prevailing military ideal was that of the armed mob or crowd—a body of fighters following a chosen leader against Indians.

ENGLAND AND AMERICA 219

Everywhere the elementary conceptions of obedience and duty were unknown. The very men who wished for war were unwilling to fight except on their own terms.

Still more fatal to military efficiency was the fact that the Federalists, and many of the northern Republicans, inhabiting the regions abutting on Canada, were violently opposed to the war, wished to see it fail, and were firmly resolved to do nothing to aid the administration. The utmost the Federalists would do was to defend themselves if attacked, but they would do that on their own responsibility and not under federal orders.

The only exception to this prevailing unmilitary condition was to be found in the navy, where, through cruising and through actual service against the Barbary corsairs, a genuinely trained body of officers and men had been created. Unable to do more than give a good account of themselves on the ocean in single combats, these officers found a chance on the northern lakes to display a fighting power and skill which is one of the few redeeming features of the war on the American side.

In 1812 hostilities began with a feeble attempt on the part of the United States to invade Canada, an effort whose details are of interest only in showing how impossible

220 THE WARS BETWEEN

it is for an essentially unmilitary people to improvise warfare. Congress had authorized a loan, the construction of vessels, and the enlistment of an army of 36,000 men; but the officers appointed to assemble a military force found themselves unable, after months of recruiting and working, to gather more than half that number of raw troops, with a fluctuating body of State militia. With these rudiments of a military force, attempts to " invade " Canada were made in three directions—from Detroit, from the Niagara River, and from the northern end of Lake Champlain.

To meet these movements, there were actually less than 2,300 British soldiers west of Montreal; but fortunately they were commanded by Isaac Brock, an officer of daring and an aggressive temper. He at once entered into alliance with Tecumseh and the western Indians, and thus brought to the British assistance a force of hundreds of warriors along the Ohio and Kentucky frontier. While General Hull, with about 2,000 troops, mainly volunteers from the West, marched under orders to Detroit and then, in July, invaded upper Canada, the outlying American posts at Chicago and Mackinac were either captured or destroyed by the Indians. Brock, gathering a handful of men, marched against Hull, terrified him for the safety of

ENGLAND AND AMERICA 221

his communications with the United States, forced the old man to retreat to Detroit, and finally, by advancing boldly against the slight fortifications of the post, frightened him into surrender. Hull had been set an impossible task, to conquer upper Canada with no sure means of getting reinforcements or supplies through a region swarming with Indians; but his conduct indicated no spark of pugnacity, and his surrender caused the loss of the entire north-west. Tecumseh and his warriors now advanced against the Kentucky, Indiana, and Ohio frontiers; and the nameless horrors of Indian massacre and torture surged along the line of settlements. The frontiersmen flew to arms. General Harrison, with a commission from Kentucky, headed a large expedition to regain lost ground; but he only succeeded in building forts in north-western Ohio and waging a defensive war against the raids of Tecumseh and the British general, Proctor, Brock's successor.

At Niagara, no move was made until the late autumn, when two American generals in succession—Van Rensselaer and Smyth—tried to lead a motley array of militia and regulars across the river. Brock met the first detachment and was killed in a skirmish, but his men were able to annihilate the main attack, on the brink of the river, while several thousand American militia, refusing, on constitutional grounds, to serve outside the jurisdiction of their state, watched safely from the eastern bank. The second effort in November, under General Smyth, proved an even worse fiasco. Meanwhile General Dearborn, the supreme commander, tried to invade near Lake Champlain; but, after he had marched his troops to the Canadian border, the militia refused to leave the soil of the United States, and so the campaign had to be abandoned. The military efforts of the United States were, as the Canadian historian phrases it, " beneath criticism."

The only redeeming feature of the year was the record of the little American navy and the success of the privateers, who rushed to prey upon British commerce. Upwards of two hundred British vessels were captured, while all but about seventy American ships reached home safely. The British sent squadrons of cruisers, but were unable to begin a blockade. Their aim was to capture American men-of-war as rapidly as possible, to prevent their doing damage, so they unhesitatingly attacked American vessels whenever they met them, regardless of slight differences in size or gun-power. The British sea-captain of the day had a hearty contempt for Americans, and never dreamed that their navy could be any more dangerous than the

ENGLAND AND AMERICA 223

French. To the unlimited delight of the American public, and the stupefaction of England, five American cruisers in succession captured or sank five British in the autumn of 1812, utilizing superior weight of broadside and more accurate gunnery with merciless severity. These blows did no actual damage to a navy which comprised several hundred frigates and sloops, but the moral effect was great. It had been proved that Americans, after all, could fight.

In 1813 there was a change in administrative officers. Doctor Eustis was replaced in the War Department by John Armstrong, who had served in the Revolution, and William Jones of Philadelphia succeeded Paul Hamilton as Secretary of the Navy. Congress authorized more men, to the number of 58,000, and more ships, and voted more loans. Finally, in the summer it was actually driven to impose internal taxes like those which, when imposed by Federalists, had savoured of tyranny.

On the northern frontier, renewed efforts were made to collect a real army, and, with late comprehension of the necessities of the case, naval officers were sent to build flotillas to control Erie, Ontario, and Champlain. On their part, the British Ministry sent out a few troops and officers to Canada, but relied this year chiefly upon a strict blockade, which was proclaimed first in December, 1812, and was extended, before the end of the year, to cover the entire coast, except New England. Ships-of-the-line, frigates, and sloops patrolled the entrances to all the seaports, terminating not only foreign but coastwise commerce.

Things went little if any better for the United States. The army was on paper 58,000 men; but the people of the north and west would not enlist. The utmost efforts at recruiting did not succeed in bringing one-half the nominal force into the field. The people would not take the war seriously, and the administration was helpless. To make matters worse, not only did the north-western frontier agonize under Indian warfare, but the south-west became involved, when, in August, 1813, the Creek Indians, affected by Tecumseh's influence, rose and began a war in Tennessee and Georgia. For months Andrew Jackson, General of Tennessee militia, with other local commanders, carried on an exhausting and murderous conflict in the swamps and woods of the south-west. The war was now assuming the character of the last stand of the Indians before the oncoming whites.

In the north-west, decisive blows were struck in this year by General Harrison and

ENGLAND AND AMERICA 225

Commander Perry. The latter built a small fleet of boats, carrying in all fifty-four guns, and sailed out to contest the control of Lake Erie. Captain Barclay, the British commander, with scantier resources, constructed a weaker fleet, with sixty-three lighter guns, and gallantly awaited the Americans on September 9. In a desperately fought battle, Perry's sloop, the *Lawrence*, was practically destroyed by the concentrated fire of the British; but the greater gun-power of the Americans told, and the entire British flotilla was compelled to surrender. This enabled Harrison, who had been waiting for months in his fortifications, to advance and pursue Proctor into upper Canada. On October 5 he brought him to action near the river Thames, winning a complete victory and killing Tecumseh. The Americans then returned to Detroit, and the Indian war gradually simmered down, until in August, 1814, the leading tribes made peace. To the eastward no such decisive action took place. Sir James Yeo and Commodore Chauncey, commanding the British and American vessels respectively on Lake Ontario, were each unwilling to risk a battle without a decisive superiority; and the result was that no serious engagement occurred. This rendered it impossible for either side to attain any military success in that region; and so the year 1813 shows only a succession of raids, a species of activity in which the British proved much the more daring and efficient. During one of these affairs, General Dearborn occupied the Canadian town of York, now Toronto, and burned the public buildings—an act of needless destruction for which the United States was destined to pay heavily. Further eastward, General Wilkinson and General Hampton began a joint invasion of lower Canada, Wilkinson leading a force of over 6,000 men down the St. Lawrence, Hampton advancing with 4,000 from Lake Champlain toward the same goal, Montreal. But at Chrystler's Farm, on November 11, the rearguard of Wilkinson's army suffered a thorough defeat at the hands of a small pursuing force; and Hampton underwent a similar repulse from an inferior body of French-Canadians under Colonel de Salaberry, at Chateauguy, on October 25. Finally, Hampton, suspecting that Armstrong and Wilkinson intended in case of any failure to throw the blame on him, decided to withdraw, November 11, and Wilkinson followed. The whole invasion came to an inglorious conclusion.

At sea the uniform success of American cruisers came to a stop, for, out of four naval duels, two were British victories, notably the taking of the unlucky *Chesapeake* by the

Shannon. Only where privateers and sloops swept West Indian waters and hung about British convoys was there much to satisfy American feelings; and all the while the blockading squadrons cruised at their ease in Chesapeake and Delaware bays and Long Island Sound. The country was now subjected to increasing distress from the stoppage of all commerce; not only was the Federal government sorely pinched from loss of tariff revenue, but the New England towns suffered from starvation prices for food products, while in the middle and southern States grain was used to feed the cattle or allowed to rot.

For the season of 1814, it was necessary again to try to build up armies; and now the time was growing short during which the United States could hope to draw advantage from the preoccupation of England in the European struggle. During the winter of 1814, the final crushing of Napoleon took place, ending with his abdication and the restoration of the Bourbons. Simultaneously, the British campaign in Spain was carried to its triumphant conclusion, and after April British armies had no further European occupation. Unless peace were made, or unless the United States gained such advantages in Canada as to render the British ready to treat, it was practically certain that the summer would find the full power of the British army, as well as the navy, in a position to be directed against the American frontier and the American sea-coast.

Congress, however, did nothing new. It authorized a loan, raised the bounty for enlistments, voted a further increase of the army, and adjourned. Armstrong, the Secretary of War, succeeded in replacing the worn-out veterans who had mismanaged the campaigns of 1812–1813 with fighting generals, younger men, such as Jacob Brown, Scott, Ripley, and Jackson, the Indian fighter; but he could not induce men to enlist any more freely, nor did he show any ability in planning operations. So events dragged on much as before.

On Lake Ontario, Chauncey and Yeo continued their cautious policy, building vessels continually and never venturing out of port unless for the moment in overwhelming force. The result was that first one then the other controlled the lake; but they never met. The only serious fighting took place near Niagara, where General Brown, with a little force of 2,600 men, tried to invade Canada, and was met first by General Riall, and later by General Drummond, with practically equal forces. Here the Americans actually fought, and fought hard, winning a slight success at Chippawa on July 5, and engaging

ENGLAND AND AMERICA

in a drawn battle at Lundy's Lane on July 25. Later forced to take refuge in Fort Erie, Brown made a successful defence against Drummond, and obliged him to abandon an effort at siege. Here, as in the naval combats, the military showing of the Americans was at last creditable; but the campaign was on too trivial a scale to produce any results. In the south-west this year, Jackson pushed through his attack on the Creeks to a triumphant conclusion, and in spite of mutinous militia and difficult forests compelled the Indians on August 9, 1814, to purchase peace by large cessions of land.

By the middle of the summer, however, the British were ready to lay a heavy hand on the United States and punish the insolent country for its annoying attack in the rear. New England was now subjected to the blockade, and troops from Wellington's irresistible army were sent across, some to the squadron in the Chesapeake, others to Canada, and later still others in a well-equipped expedition to New Orleans to conquer the mouth of the Mississippi.

The Chesapeake squadron, after raiding and provisioning itself at the expense of the Virginia and Maryland farmers, made a dash at Washington, sending boats up the Patuxent and Potomac rivers, and landing a body of about 2,000 men. On August 24, with absurd ease, this force scattered in swift panic a hasty collection of militia, and entered Washington, sending the President and Cabinet flying into the country. In retaliation for the damage done at York, the British officers set fire to the capital and other public buildings, before retreating swiftly to their ships. A similar attack on Baltimore, September 11, was better met, and, although the British routed a force of militia, the attempt to take the city was abandoned. The humiliation of the capture of Washington led to the downfall of Armstrong as Secretary of War, although not until after he had almost ruined another campaign.

While the British were threatening Washington, another force was gathering north of Lake Champlain, and a large frigate was being built to secure command of that lake. By the end of August, nearly 16,000 men, most of them from Wellington's regiments, were assembled to invade New York, probably with the intention of securing the permanent occupation of the northern part. In the face of this, Armstrong sent most of the American troops at Plattsburg on a useless march across New York State, leaving a bare handful under General McComb to meet the invasion. When Sir George Prevost, Governor-General of Canada, advanced to Plattsburg on September 6, he found nothing but militia and volunteers before him. Fortunately for the United States, Prevost was no fighter, and he declined to advance or attack unless he had a naval control of the lake. On September 11 the decisive contest took place. McDonough, the American commander, with a small squadron, entirely defeated and captured the British flotilla under Downie. It was Lake Erie over again, with the difference that in this battle the American fleet was not superior to the British. It was a victory due to better planning and better gunnery, and it led to the immediate retreat of Prevost, who tamely abandoned the whole campaign, to the intense mortification of his officers and men. The remaining expedition, under General Pakenham, comprising 16,000 Peninsular veterans, under convoy of a strong fleet, sailed to the Gulf of Mexico and advanced to capture New Orleans. General Andrew Jackson was at hand, and with him a mass of militia and frontiersmen. Driven by the furious energy of the Indian fighter, the Americans showed aggressiveness and courage in skirmishes and night attacks, and finally won an astounding victory on January 8, 1815. On that day the British force tried to storm, by frontal attack, a line of intrenchments armed with cannon and packed with riflemen. In twenty-five minutes their columns were so badly cut up by grapeshot and musketry that the whole attack was abandoned, after Pakenham himself had been killed. The expedition withdrew, and sailing to Mobile, a town in Spanish territory, occupied by the Americans, retook it on February 11; but the main purpose of their invasion was foiled.

In this year, while American land forces struggled to escape destruction, the naval vessels were for the most part shut in by the blockade. Occasional captures were still made in single combat; but British frigates were now under orders to refuse battle with the larger American vessels, and the captures by sloops were counterbalanced by the British capture of the frigate *Essex* by two antagonists in March, 1814. Practically the only extensive operations carried on were by American privateers, who now haunted the British Channel and captured merchantmen within sight of the English coasts. The irritation caused by these privateers was excessive, and made British shipowners and merchants anxious for peace; but it had no effect on the military situation. England was not to be subdued by mere annoyance.

By the end of 1814, the time seemed to be at hand when the United States must submit to peace on such terms as England chose to dictate, or risk disruption and ruin. The administrative weaknesses of the country culminated in actual financial bankruptcy, which was due in no small part to the fact that Federalist financiers and bankers, determining to do all the damage possible, steadily refused to subscribe to the loans or to give any assistance. The powerful New England capital was entirely withheld. The result was that the strain on the rest of the banks became too great; and after the capture of Washington they all suspended specie payment, leaving the Government only the notes of suspended banks, or its own depreciated treasury notes for currency. All the coin in the country steadily flowed into the vaults of New England banks, while the Federal Treasury was compelled, on November 9, 1814, to admit its inability to pay interest on its loans. Congress met in the autumn and endeavoured to remedy the situation by chartering a bank; but under the general suspension of specie payments it was impossible to start one solvent from the beginning. When Congress authorized one without power to suspend specie payments, Madison vetoed it as useless. All that could be done was to issue more treasury notes. As for the army, a Bill for compulsory service was brought in, showing the enormous change in Republican ideals; but it failed to pass. Congress seemed helpless. The American people would neither enlist for the war nor authorize their representatives to pass genuine war measures.

The Federalists, controlling most of the New England States, now felt that the time had come to insist on a termination of their grievances. Their governors had refused to allow militia to assist, their legislatures had done nothing to aid the war; their capitalists had declined to subscribe, and their farmers habitually sold provisions to the British over the Canadian boundary, actually supplying Sir George Prevost's army by contract. There met, at Hartford, on December 14, 1814, a convention of leading men, officially or unofficially representing the five New England States, who agreed upon a document which was intended to secure the special rights of their region. They demanded amendments to the Constitution abolishing the reckoning of slaves as basis for congressional representation, providing for the partial distribution of government revenues among the States, prohibiting embargoes or commercial warfare, or the election of successive Presidents from the same State, and requiring a two-thirds vote of Congress to admit new States or declare war. This was meant for an ultimatum; and it was generally understood that, if the Federal government did not submit to these terms, the New England States would secede to rid themselves of what they considered the intolerable oppression of Virginian misgovernment.

Such was the state of things in the winter of 1815. The administration of Madison had utterly failed to secure any of the ends of the war, to inflict punishment on Great Britain, or to conquer Canada. It had also utterly failed to maintain financial solvency, to enlist an army, to create a navy capable of keeping the sea, or to prevent a movement in New England which seemed to be on the verge of breaking the country into pieces. But to lay this miserable failure— for such only can it be called—to the personal discredit of Jefferson and Madison is unfair, for it was only the repetition under new governmental conditions of the old traditional colonial method of carrying on war as a local matter. The French and Indian War, the Revolution, and the War of 1812, repeated in different generations the same tale of amateur warfare, of the occasional success and usual worthlessness of the militia, the same administrative inefficiency, and the same financial breakdown. Without authority and obedience, there can be carried on no real war; and authority and obedience were no more known and no better appreciated in 1812 than they had been in the days of Washington. Jefferson, Madison, and their party had gone with the current of American tradition; that was their only fault.

CHAPTER XII

END OF THE ANTAGONISM: A CENTURY OF PEACE

WHEN the American war began, the English showed a tendency to blame the Tory administration for permitting it to take place; but the chief feeling, after all, was one of annoyance at Madison and his party for having decided to give their assistance to Napoleon at the crisis of his career. The intercourse between Englishmen and New England Federalists had given British society its understanding of American politics and coloured its natural irritation toward the Republican administration with something of the deeper venom of the outraged New Englanders, who saw in Jefferson and his successors a race of half-Jacobins. During 1812 and 1813, accordingly, newspapers and ministerial speakers, when they referred to the contest, generally spoke of the necessity of chastising an impudent and presumptuous antagonist. A friendly party such as had defended the colonists during the Revolution no longer existed, for the Whigs, however antagonistic to the Liverpool Ministry, were fully as firmly committed to maintaining British naval and commercial supremacy.

England's chief continental ally, however, the Tsar Alexander, considered the American war an unfortunate blunder; and, as early as September, 1812, he offered his mediation through young John Quincy Adams, Minister at St. Petersburg. The news reached America in March, 1813, and Madison revealed his willingness to withdraw from a contest already shown to be unprofitable by immediately accepting and nominating Adams, with Bayard and Gallatin, to serve as peace commissioners. Without waiting to hear from England, these envoys started for Russia, but reached there only to meet an official refusal on the part of England, dated July 5, 1813. The Liverpool Ministry did not wish to have the American war brought within the range of European consideration, since its settlement under such circumstances might raise questions of neutral rights which would be safer out of the hands of a Tsar whose predecessors had framed armed neutralities in 1780 and 1801. Accordingly, the British government intimated politely that it would be willing to deal directly with the United States, and thus waved the unwelcome Russian mediation aside. Madison accepted this offer in March, 1814; but, although the American commissioners endeavoured through Alexander Baring, their friend and defender in Parliament, to get the British government to appoint a time and place for meeting, they encountered continued delays.

A considerable element in the Tory party felt that the time had come to inflict a severe punishment upon the United States, and newspapers and speakers of that connection announced freely that only by large concessions of territory could the contemptible republic purchase peace. When the Ministry finally sent commissioners to Ghent, on August 8, 1814, it was not with any expectation of coming to a prompt agreement, but merely to engage the Americans while the various expeditions then under way took Washington and Baltimore, occupied northern New York, and captured New Orleans. It was generally expected that a few months would find large portions of the United States in British possession, as was in fact the seacoast of Maine, east of Penobscot Bay, after September first.

The instructions to the British peace commissioners were based on the *uti pos-*

sedetis, as the British government intended it to be by the end of the year, when they expected to hold half of Maine, the northern parts of New York, New Hampshire and Vermont, the north-western post of Mackinnac, and possibly New Orleans and Mobile. In addition, there was to be an Indian territory established under British guarantee west of the old treaty line of 1795, and all American fishing rights were to be terminated. On the other side, the American instructions, while hinting that England would do well to cede Canada, made the abandonment of the alleged right of impressments by England a *sine quâ non*. Clearly no agreement between such points of view was possible; and the outcome of the negotiation was bound to depend on the course of events in the United States. The first interviews resulted in revealing that part of the British instructions related to the Indian territory with intimations of coming demands for territorial cessions. This the Americans instantly rejected on August 25, and the negotiation came to a standstill for several weeks.

The three British negotiators, Admiral Gambier, Henry Goulburn, and Doctor Adams were men of slight political or personal authority, and their part consisted chiefly in repeating their instructions and referring American replies back to Lord Castlereagh, the Foreign Secretary, or to Lord Bathurst, who acted as his substitute while he attended the Congress of Vienna. The American commissioners, including the three original ones, Adams, Bayard, and Gallatin, to whom Clay and Russell of Massachusetts were now added, clearly understood the situation, and had already warned Madison that an insistence on the abandonment of impressments would result in the failure to secure any treaty. In October, 1814, a despatch yielded this point and left the negotiators to make the best fight they could, unhampered by positive instructions. Undoubtedly they would have been compelled to submit to hard terms, in spite of their personal ability, which stood exceedingly high, had not news of the repulse at Baltimore, of the treaty of July, 1814, by which the north-western Indians agreed to fight the English, and, on October 17, of the retreat of Sir George Prevost after the defeat of Plattsburg, come in to change the situation.

Between August and October little had been accomplished, during a slow interchange of notes, beyond a withdrawal by the British of their demand for an Indian territory, and an acceptance in its place of an agreement to include the Indians in a general peace. Then the Cabinet, seeing that after Prevost's retreat they could no longer claim the terri-

ENGLAND AND AMERICA 241

tory outlined in the first instructions, authorized the negotiators to demand only Mackinac and Niagara, with a right of way across Maine. The Americans, encouraged by the news from Plattsburg, replied on October 23, refusing to treat on the *uti possedetis*, or on any terms but the *status quo ante*. This brought the Tory government face to face with the question whether the war was to be continued for another year for the purpose of conquering a frontier for Canada; and, before the prospect of continued war taxation, annoyance from privateers, and a doubtful outcome, they hesitated. Turning to Wellington for a decision, they asked him whether he would accept the command in America for the purpose of conquering a peace. His reply showed little interest or desire to go, although he seemed confident of success; but he observed that, on the basis of the military situation, they had no right to demand any territorial cession.

The Ministry then, on November 18, definitely abandoned the claim for compensation, and accepted as a basis for discussion a plan submitted by the American commissioners. In the preparation of this a sharp quarrel had broken out between Clay, who insisted on terminating the British right to navigate the Mississippi, and Adams, who demanded the retention of the American right to fish in Canadian waters. Gallatin pointed out that the two privileges stood together, and with great difficulty he induced the two men to agree to the omission of both matters from the treaty, although Clay refused until the last to sign. So the commission presented a united front in offering to renew both rights or postpone them for discussion; and the British commissioners finally accepted the latter alternative. The treaty was then signed in the old Carthusian Convent at Ghent, on December 24, 1814, as a simple cessation of hostilities and return to the *status quo ante* as regards conquests. Not a word related to any of the numerous causes of the war. Impressments, blockades, Orders in Council, the Indian relations, the West Indian trade rights,—all were abandoned. So far as the United States was concerned the treaty was an acknowledgment of defeat, a recognition that the war was a failure.

In view of the hopes of Canadian gains, the treaty was denounced in England by the Opposition journals and many of those most antagonistic to America as a cowardly surrender. But it was none the less heartily accepted by both peoples and both governments. It reached the United States on February 11, was sent to the Senate on February 15, and ratified unanimously the next day. There

ENGLAND AND AMERICA 243

still remained various vessels at sea, and so the winter of 1815 saw not only the amazing victory of Jackson at New Orleans, but also several naval actions, in which the United States frigate *President* was taken by a squadron of British blockades, two American sloops in duels took two British smaller vessels, and the American *Constitution*, in a night action, captured, together, two British sloops. Then the news spread, and peace finally arrived in fact.

In England, the whole affair was quickly forgotten in the tremendous excitement caused by the return of Napoleon from Elba, the uprising of Europe, and the dramatic meeting of the two great captains, Wellington and Napoleon, in the Waterloo campaign. By the time the Napoleonic Empire had finally collapsed, the story of the American war, with its maritime losses and scanty land triumphs, was an old one, and the British exporters, rushing to regain their former markets, were happy in the prospect of the reopening of American ports. By October, trade relations were re-established and the solid intercourse of the two countries was under way.

In America all disgraces and defeats were forgotten in the memories of New Orleans, Plattsburg, and Chippawa, and the people at large, willing to forgive all its failures to the

Republican administration, resumed with entire contentment the occupations of peace. The war fabric melted like a cloud; armies were disbanded, vessels were called home, credit rose, prices sprang upward, importations swelled, exportation began.

In truth, the time of antagonism was at an end, for, with the European peace of 1814, the immediate cause for irritation was removed, never to return. The whole structure of blockades, Orders in Council, seizures, and restrictions upon neutrals vanished; the necessity for British impressments ceased to exist; and, since France never again came into hostility with England, none of these grievances were revived. But in a broader way the year 1815 and the decades following marked the end of national hostility, for the fundamental antagonisms which, since 1763, had repeatedly brought about irritation and conflict, began after this time to die out.

In the first place, the defeat of the Indians in the war allowed the people of the United States to advance unchecked into the north-west and south-west, filling the old Indian lands, and rendering any continuation of the restrictive diplomacy on the part of England for the benefit of Canadian fur traders patently futile. The war was no sooner ended than roads, trails, and rivers swarmed

ENGLAND AND AMERICA 245

with westward-moving emigrants; and within a year the territory of Indiana, which the British commissioners at Ghent had wished to establish as an Indian reserve, was framing a State constitution. In 1818 Illinois followed.

The revulsion of temper was illustrated in the commencement at this time of the organized movement for settled international peace, which may be dated from the establishment of the New York and Massachusetts Peace Societies in 1815, and the London Peace Society in the following year. But its most signal expression came in the remarkable agreement by which the Canadian-American frontier has been, for nearly a century, unfortified, and yet completely peaceful. On November 16, 1815, State Secretary Monroe instructed Adams to propose to the British Government that—as, " if each party augments its force there with a view to obtaining the ascendancy over the other, vast expense will be incurred and the danger of collision augmented in like degree "—such military preparations should be suspended on both sides. The smaller the number of the armed forces agreed upon, he said, the better; " or to abstain altogether from an armed force beyond that used for the revenue." After some suspicious hesitation, Lord Castlereagh accepted this novel proposal; and it was given effect to by an exchange of notes, signed by Mr. Bagot, British Minister at Washington, and Mr. Rush (Monroe's successor) on April 28 and 29, 1817, approved by the Senate a year later, and proclaimed by the President on April 28, 1818. By Rush-Bagot Agreement, the naval force of each Government was limited to one small gun-boat of each power on Champlain and Ontario, and two on the upper lakes, an arrangement of immense value to both Canada and the United States.

The old-time commercial antagonism was also destined to disappear in a few years after the close of the war. At first England clung to the time-honoured West Indian policy, and, when in 1815 the two countries adjusted their commercial relations, American vessels were still excluded, although given the right to trade directly with the East Indies. But already the new economic thought, which regarded competition and reciprocal trade as the ideal, instead of legal discriminations and universal protectionism, was gaining ground, as England became more and more the manufacturing centre of the world. Under Huskisson, in 1825, reciprocity was definitely substituted for exclusion; and a few years later, under Peel and Russell, and within the lifetime of men who had maintained the Orders in Council, the whole

ENGLAND AND AMERICA 247

elaborate system of laws backed by the logic of Lord Sheffield and James Stephen was cast away and fell into disrepute and oblivion.

In America, it should be added, the rush of settlers into the West and the starting of manufactures served, within a few years from the end of the War of 1812, to alter largely the former dependence of the United States upon foreign commerce. By the time that England was ready to abandon its restrictive policy, the United States was beginning to be a manufacturing nation with its chief wealth in its great internal trade, and the ancient interest in the West Indies was fast falling into insignificance. The same men who raged against the Jay treaty and the Orders in Council lived to forget that they had ever considered the West India trade important. So, on both sides, the end of commercial antagonism was soon to follow on the Treaty of Ghent.

Finally, and more slowly, the original political and social antagonism ceased to be active, and ultimately died out. So far as the United States was concerned, the change was scarcely visible until three-quarters of a century after the Treaty of Ghent. The temper of the American people, formed by Revolutionary traditions and nourished on memories of battle and injuries, remained steadily antagonistic toward England; and the triumph of western social ideals served to emphasize the distinction between the American democrat and the British aristocrat, until dislike became a tradition and a political and literary convention. But the emptiness of this normal national hatred of John Bull was shown in 1898, when, at the first distinct sign of friendliness on the part of the British government and people, the whole American anglophobia vanished, and the people of the continent realized that the time had come for a recognition of the essential and normal harmony of the ancient enemies.

In England, the change began somewhat earlier, for within less than a generation after the Treaty of Ghent the exclusive Tory control collapsed, and the Revolution of 1832 gave the middle classes a share of political power. A few years later the Radicals, representing the working-men, became a distinct force in Parliament, and to middle class and Radicals there was nothing abhorrent in the American Republic. Aristocratic society continued, of course, as in the eighteenth century, to regard the United States with scant respect, and those members of the upper middle classes who took their social tone from the aristocracy commonly reflected their prejudices. But the masses of the British people—whose relatives emigrated steadily to the western land of promise—felt a genuine sympathy and interest in the success of the great democratic experiment, a sympathy which was far deeper and more effective than had been that of the the eighteenth-century Whigs. From the moment that these classes made their weight felt in government, the time was at hand when the old social antagonism was to die out, and with it the deep political antipathy which, since the days of 1793, had tinged the official British opinion of a democratic state. The last evidence of the Tory point of view came when, in 1861, the American Civil War brought out the unconcealed aversion of the British nobility and aristocracy for the northern democracy; but on the occasion the equally unconcealed sense of political and social sympathy manifested by the British middle and working classes served to prevent any danger to the United States, and to keep England from aiding in the disruption of the Union.

Thus the Treaty of Ghent, marking the removal of immediate causes of irritation, was the beginning of a period in which the underlying elements of antagonism between England and the United States were definitely to cease. When every discount is made, the celebration, heartily supported by the national leaders on both sides, of a century of peace between the British, Canadian, and American peoples, does exhibit, in Sir Wilfred Laurier's words, " a spectacle to astound the world by its novelty and grandeur."

BIBLIOGRAPHY

The references to the epoch covered in this volume may be rather sharply divided into those which deal with the years before 1783, and those which relate to the subsequent period. In the first group, there are both British and American works of high excellence, but in the second there are practically none but American authorities, owing to the preoccupation of British writers with the more dramatic and important French revolutionary and Napoleonic wars, or the events of parliamentary politics.

For the years 1763–1783 the best American history is E. CHANNING, *History of the United States*, vol. iii (1912), distinctly independent, thorough, and impartial. S. G. FISHER, *The Struggle for American Independence*, 2 vols. (1908), is cynically critical and unconventional. Three volumes of the *American Nation* series,—G. E. HOWARD, *Preliminaries of the Revolution ;* C. H. VAN TYNE, *The American Revolution ;* and A. C. MCLAUGHLIN, *The Confederation and the Constitution* (1905), are equally scholarly and less detailed. The older American works, exhibiting the traditional "patriotic" view, are best represented by J. FISKE, *American Revolution*, 2 vols. (1891); and G. BANCROFT, *History of the United States*, 6 vols. (ed. 1883–1885).

On the English side the most valuable study is in W. E. H. LECKY, *England in the Eighteenth Century*, vols. iii, iv (1878), a penetrating and impartial analysis. The Whig view appears in SIR G. O. TREVELYAN, *The American Revolution*, 3 vols. (1899–1907); LORD MAHON, *England in the Eighteenth Century*, vols. v–vii (1853–1854); and M. MARKS, *England and America*, 2 vols. (1907), while W. HUNT, *Political History*, 1760–1801 (1905), alone of recent writers, presents a Tory version of events.

Special works of value are C. STEDMAN, *The American War*, 2 vols. (1794), the authoritative English contemporary account of military events, and, among recent studies, J. W. FORTESCUE, *History of the British Army*, vol. iii (1902), which should be compared with H. B. CARRINGTON, *Battles of the Revolution* (1876); E. MCCRADY, *South Carolina in the Revolution*, 2 vols. (1901–2); E. J. LOWELL, *The Hessians in the*

Revolution (1884); J. B. PERKINS, *France in the American Revolution* (1911); C. H. VAN TYNE, *The Loyalists* (1902), and W. HERTZ, *The Old Colonial System* (1905). Of especial value are the destructive criticisms in C. F. ADAMS, *Studies Military and Diplomatic* (1911). The authoritative treatment of naval history is found in A. T. MAHAN, *Influence of Sea Power* (1890), and in the chapter by the same writer in W. L. CLOWES, *History of the Royal Navy*, vols. iii, iv (1898–1899).

Among leading biographies are those of Washington by H. C. LODGE (2 vols. 1890), by W. C. FORD (2 vols. 1900), and by GEN. B. T. JOHNSON (1894); of Franklin by J. PARTON (2 vols. 1864), by J. BIGELOW (3 vols. 1874), and by J. T. MORSE (1889); of Henry by M. C. TYLER (1887); of Samuel Adams by J. K. HOSMER (1885); of Robert Morris by E. P. OBERHOLZER (1903), and of Steuben by F. KAPP (1859). On the English side the *Memoirs of Horace Walpole* (1848); the *Correspondence of George III with Lord North*, ed. by W. B. DONNE (1867), are valuable and interesting, and some material may be found in the lives of Burke by T. McKNIGHT (2 vols. 1858); of Shelburne by E. G. FITZMAURICE (2 vols. 1875); of Chatham by F. HARRISON (1905) and A. VON RUVILLE (3 vols. 1907); and of Fox by LORD JOHN RUSSELL (3 vols. 1859). The biographies of two governors of Massachusetts, C. A. POWNALL, *Thomas Pownall* (1908), and J. K. HOSMER, *Thomas Hutchinson* (1896), are of value as presenting the colonial Tory point of view.

For the period after 1783, the best reference book and the only one which attempts to trace in detail the motives of British as well as American statesmen is HENRY ADAMS, *History of the United States*, 9 vols. (1891). It is impartially critical, in a style of sustained and caustic vivacity. Almost equally valuable is A. T. MAHAN, *Sea Power in Relation to the War of 1812*, 2 vols. (1905), which contains the only sympathetic analysis of British naval and commercial policy, 1783–1812, beside being the authoritative work on naval events. The standard American works are J. SCHOULER, *History of the United States*, vols. i, ii (1882); J. B. McMASTER, *History of the People of the United States*, vols. i–iv (1883–1895); R. HILDRETH, *History of the United States*, vols. ii–vi (1849–1852), and three volumes of the *American Nation Series*, J. S. BASSETT, *The Federalist System ;* E. CHANNING, *The Jeffersonian System*, and K. C. BABCOCK, *Rise of American Nationality* (1906). On the English side there is little in the general histories beyond a chapter on American relations in A. ALISON, *Modern Europe*, vol. iv (1848), which accurately represents the extreme Tory contempt for the United States, but has no other merit. Works on Canadian history fill this

BIBLIOGRAPHY 253

gap to a certain extent, such as W. KINGSFORD, *History of Canada*, vol. viii (1895).

Beside the work of Mahan (as above) the War of 1812 is dealt with by W. JAMES, *Naval History of Great Britain*, vols. v–vi (1823), a work of accuracy as to British facts, but of violent anti-American temper; and on the other side by J. F. COOPER, *Naval History* (1856), and T. ROOSEVELT, *Naval War of 1812* (1883). Sundry special works dealing with economic and social questions involved in international relations are T. ROOSEVELT, *Winning of the West*, 4 vols. (1899–1902); W. CUNNINGHAM, *Growth of English Industry and Commerce*, vol. iii (1893), and W. SMART, *Economic Annals of the Nineteenth Century* (1910). Biographical material is to be found, in the lives of Washington (as above); of Jefferson by J. SCHOULER, (1897), and by J. T. MORSE (1883); of Hamilton by J. T. MORSE (1882), and F. S. OLIVER (1907); of Gallatin by H. ADAMS (1879); of Madison by G. HUNT (1903); of Josiah Quincy by E. QUINCY (1869). There is some biographical material to be found in BROUGHAM'S *Life and Times of Lord Brougham*, vol. iii (1872), and in S. WALPOLE, *Life of Spencer Perceval*, 2 vols. (1874), but for the most part the British version of relations with America after 1783 is still to be discovered only in the contemporary sources such as the *Parliamentary History* and *Debates*, the *Annual Register*, and the partly published papers of such leaders as Pitt, Fox, Grenville, Canning, Castlereagh and Perceval.

A useful sketch, giving prominence to the Treaty of Ghent and the Rush-Bagot Agreement, and summarizing earlier and later events, is *A Short History of Anglo-American Relations and of the Hundred Years' Peace*, by H. S. PERRIS.

Documents and other contemporary material for the whole period may be conveniently found in W. MACDONALD, *Select Charters* (1904) and *Select Documents* (1898); in G. CALLENDER, *Economic History of the United States* (1909), and A. B. HART, *American History told by Contemporaries*, vols. ii, iii (1898, 1901).

INDEX

ADAMS, JOHN, in Revolution, 48, 57, 63, 71, 118–125; after 1783, 142, 147, 155, 173–180
Adams, John Quincy, 237–241
Adams, Samuel, 32, 42, 50, 57, 63, 78, 131, 144
Adet, P. A., 172, 173
Alexander I, 190, 237
Alien and Sedition Acts, 176–180
Anti-Federalists, 143, 147
Armstrong, John, 223–230
Arnold, Benedict, 67, 81, 85, 104

Baltimore, 84, 230, 238, 240
Bank of the United States, 145, 146, 183, 218
Banks, State, 218, 233
Baring, Alexander, 212, 238
Bayard, James A., 237, 240
Beaumarchais, Caron de, 94
Bedford, Duke of, 46
Bonaparte, Napoleon, 179, 184–186, 189–198, 202–208, 213–216, 227, 236, 243
Brock, General Isaac, 220, 221
Brougham, Henry, 212
Brown, General Jacob, 228, 229
Bunker Hill, Battle of, 65, 66, 78, 83
Burgoyne, General John, 89–95, 113, 114
Burke, Edmund, 52, 60, 68, 73, 74, 96, 115, 116, 161, 165
Burr, Aaron, 179, 180

Camden, Battle of, 103
Canada, British policy in, 29, 54, 67, 73, 81, 85, 100, 119, 122, 127, 155, 158, 200, 210, 211; defence of, 214–229, 239, 241, 244, 245
Canning, George, 197, 202, 204, 205, 207, 212
Carleton, General Guy, 81, 85, 158

Chauncey, Commodore Isaac, 225, 228
Clark, George Rogers, 101, 105
Clay, Henry, 211, 214, 240, 241
Clinton, De Witt, 214
Clinton, George, 147, 169
Clinton, Sir Henry, 92, 100–103, 109–113
Concord, Battle of, 62, 78
Confederation, Articles of, 105, 129–136
Congress, Continental, 56, 57, 60, 63, 64, 71, 79, 80, 84, 88–93, 98, 105, 118, 130
Congress of the Confederation, 107, 124, 125, 127, 130–138, 142, 157
Congress, United States, under Federalists, 140–146, 155, 164, 173, 175, 177; under Republicans, 182, 186, 187, 195, 199–209, 211, 213, 220, 223, 228, 233, 234
Constitution, United States, 139–141, 159, 180, 183, 234
Cornwallis, Lord, 86, 103–114

Dartmouth, Earl of, 47, 50
Declaration of Independence, 71, 98
De Grasse, Admiral, 110–112, 125
D'Estaing, Admiral, 100–102
Dickinson, John, 42, 50, 57, 64, 105

Elections, Presidential, 142, 147, 173, 178–180, 187, 201, 214
Erie, Lake, Battle of, 225
Erskine, David M., 204, 205

Fauchet, J. A., 163, 172
Finances, of Revolution, 16, 64, 106, 123, 124, 133–135, 144–146, 182, 191, 218–220, 228, 233

INDEX 255

Fox, Charles James, 96, 115–121, 152, 153, 165, 193
Franklin, Benjamin, in England, 38, 44, 51, 52, 64; in France, 71, 83, 93–95, 107, 118–124

Gage, General Thomas, 58, 61, 65
Gallatin, Albert, 182, 237, 240, 242
Gates, General Horatio, 79, 90, 91, 93, 103
Genet, Edmond C., 161–163
Germaine, Lord George, 53, 76, 77, 88, 115
Governors, Colonial, 15–17, 26, 27, 44, 62, 72
Grafton, Duke of, 39, 40, 47
Greene, General Nathaniel, 79, 84, 104, 109
Grenville, George, 28, 30, 31, 35, 45, 53
Grenville, William, Lord, 165, 166, 171, 193, 194, 198, 203

Hamilton, Alexander, 132, 135, 144–148, 162, 164, 168, 177, 179, 180, 188
Harrison, General W. H., 210, 211, 221–225
Hartford Convention, 234
Henry, Patrick, 32, 42, 50, 57, 78, 131, 144
Hillsborough, Lord, 43–53
Howe, Admiral, 82, 83, 100, 114
Howe, General Sir William, 82–92, 95, 113, 114
Hull, General William, 220
Hutchinson, Governor Thomas, 49, 52

Indians, of Northwest, 29, 100, 157–159, 164, 168, 209–213, 218–225, 239, 244, 245
Indians, Southwestern, 157, 210, 224, 229

Jackson, Andrew, 224, 228, 229, 231, 243
Jay, John, 42, 57, 118, 120–125, 156, 157, 165–167, 171
Jefferson, Thomas, 71, 78, 144, 146, 147, 156, 161, 169, 172, 178, 180, 181–188, 193–196, 199–203, 209, 213, 215, 217, 235, 236

King's Mountain, Battle of, 104

Lafayette, Marquis de, 102
Lee, General Charles, 79, 84, 99
Lee, Richard Henry, 57, 144

Livingston, Robert R., 125, 186
Long Island, Battle of, 83
Louis XVI, 93, 95, 156

Madison, James, 132, 135, 142, 144, 146, 147, 163, 164, 172, 178, 193, 201–208, 213–215, 230, 233–238, 240
Ministries, British, Bute, 35, 40; Grenville, 28, 35, 43; First Rockingham, 36, 39; Grafton, 39–45; North, 47–56, 60, 68–77, 88, 95–98, 114–117, 151; Second Rockingham, 117, 120; Shelburne, 120–123, 126, 152–154; Coalition, 126, 153, 154; Pitt, 152–154, 159, 162–167, 171; Addington, 171; Second Pitt, 171, 192, 193; Lord Grenville, 193, 196, 197; Portland, 197, 202, 207; Perceval, 207, 211–215; Liverpool, 212, 213, 237–241
Monroe, James, 172, 173, 186, 196
Montgomery, General Richard, 67, 79
Morgan, Daniel, 67, 68, 90, 104
Morris, Robert, 78, 107, 134

Navigation Acts, 22–25, 29, 38, 55, 72, 132, 150, 155
Non-importation Act, 196–200
Non-intercourse Act, 202, 206, 213
North, Lord, Tory leader, 43–56, 60, 61, 73–76; in Revolutionary war, 77, 97, 115–117, 153

Oswald, Richard, 119–121
Otis, James, 27, 32

Perceval, Spencer, 197, 207, 212
Perry, Commander O. H., 225
Pinckney, C. C., 173, 174
Pitt, William, Earl of Chatham, 9, 36, 38–40, 53, 60, 96–98
Pitt, William, 144, 148, 152–154, 171, 176, 189, 192
Pownall, Thomas, 41, 47, 53
Prevost, Sir George, 230, 231, 234
Proclamation of 1763, 29, 122
Proctor, Colonel Henry, 221, 225

Quebec Act, 54, 56

Randolph, Edmund, 163, 164, 172, 180, 211
Representatives, House of, 164, 180, 211
Rochambeau, Comte de, 102, 11 113

INDEX

Rockingham, Marquis of, 117, 120
Rutledge, John, 57, 78, 83

St. Clair, General Arthur, 159
St. Leger, Colonel B., 90
Sandwich, Earl of, 53, 68, 76, 77, 99, 115
Saratoga, Surrender at, 92
Scott, Sir William, 193
Secession, 188, 201, 234, 235
Sedition Act, 176–178, 180
Shays' Rebellion, 137
Sheffield, Lord, 150, 151, 154, 192, 197, 247
Shelburne, Earl of, 117, 119–123, 152–154
Sherman, Roger, 78, 135
Stamp Act, 30–33, 200
States Rights, 146, 178, 234
Stephen, James, 192, 197, 207, 247
Sugar Act, 25, 29, 31

Talleyrand, 175, 177
Tarleton, Colonel B., 103, 110
Tecumseh, 210, 211, 220, 221, 224, 225
Townshend, Charles, 40–43
Townshend Duties, 40–47, 210
Treaties, 1763, 9, 28, 1778, 95, 98; 1783, 117–127, 149–152, 158; 1794, 165–172, 193, 196; 1795, 168, 184; 1803, 186; 1814, 242; 1818, 244
Trenton, Battle of, 86, 112

Vergennes, Comte de, 93–96, 119–125

Washington, George, Commander, 42, 57, 64, 66, 79, 83–93, 99, 100, 107–112, 126; in retirement, 132, 134; President, 142, 144, 146, 147, 159, 162, 164, 167, 172–174, 178
Wayne, General Anthony, 79, 159, 164
Wellington, Duke of, 241, 243
West Indies, British, before 1783, 9, 21–27, 99, 102, 108, 110, 112, 125; after 1783, 132, 149–151, 166, 167, 246, 247
West Indies, French, trade with, 25, 27, 31, 156, 163, 167, 191–193, 196
Wilkes, John, 44, 45
Wilkinson, General James, 226

X. Y. Z. affair, 174, 175

Yorktown, Surrender at, 112, 116, 160

DAVID GLENN HUNT
MEMORIAL LIBRARY
GALVESTON COLLEGE